Mississippi

Red R.

MISSISSIPPI GEORGIA

ALABAMA

LOUISIANA

FLORIDA

Jan. 1529

FLORIDA

Currents

Tampa Bay
April 2 1528

Gulf of Mexico

Gales

CUBA

f of Campeche

YUCATAN

N

0 50 100 150 200 250 Miles

GUATEMALA

D1159929

# First Man To Cross America

# FIRST MAN TO CROSS AMERICA,

## The Story of Cabeza de Vaca

By RONALD SYME

Illustrated by
WILLIAM STOBBS

WILLIAM MORROW & COMPANY

New York, 1961

JB
N972s

Second Printing, February 1963

# CONTENTS

# First Man To Cross America

## CHAPTER 1

### *The Boy Who Read History*

THE most brilliant period of European history was just dawning when Alvar Nuñez de Vera was born in the quiet little town of Jerez, in Spain.

The year was 1493. A sea-weary little ship, with weeds and barnacles clinging to her hull, had just plodded into the mouth of Spain's

Tagus River. Her gray-bearded, gray-headed captain was hastily rowed ashore in a boat manned by excited, weather-beaten seamen. They were bringing the most wonderful news that had ever reached the Old World. The elderly sea captain, whose name was Christopher Columbus, had discovered land across the Atlantic Ocean. Three thousand miles away, declared the rumor, lay new and sunny islands which were rich in precious stones and pearls, gold, silver, and slaves.

"Any man lucky enough to reach those lands," the seamen told listeners, "can fill his pockets with gold in less time and with less trouble than it takes to weed a garden path."

When Alvar Nuñez reached the age of fifteen years, that first wild excitement in Spain had not yet died away. Indeed, the New World remained the one thought in every man's mind. Shipload after shipload of tattered and penniless Spanish adventurers were landing on the islands of the Caribbean Sea. Their greed for riches was not diminished by the fact that the promised wealth of the New World was proving uncommonly hard to find. Just enough gold and pearls and silver were being discovered to keep men's greed alive and their imaginations dreaming.

Alvar Nuñez was the only boy at his school who remained cool and almost uninterested when others discussed the search for treasure in the New World. He was a tall, slender, and rather silent youngster with thoughtful gray eyes and black, straight hair brushed back from a high forehead. The good Catholic fathers who taught the boys knew that Alvar Nuñez de Vera had the makings of a great scholar. Often they suggested to him that he should enter the Church. Curiously enough, they could never guess what he thought of the idea, for his thin-featured face was always impassive. His usual answer was courteous but indecisive.

"I have not yet considered my future," he told them. "My ancestors have been soldiers of

Spain for two hundred years, and it is a profession that has served them well. With their blood in my veins, I might not become a worthy servant of the Church."

The priests sighed as they watched Alvar Nuñez walk away. On every occasion they spoke with him, the Fathers became more certain that he had great and unusual qualities, but Alvar always remained as uncertain as the warm breeze blowing fitfully across the warm hills of southern Spain.

More than two hundred years before Alvar Nuñez de Vera was born, an ancestor of his had been a simple shepherd dwelling high in the hills of the Sierra Morena. At that period the armies of Spain were fighting an almost endless war to drive out the Moorish warriors who had invaded and settled in the southern half of the country. The shepherd guided a Spanish army across a secret pass in the mountains by a cow's skull which he had placed to mark the path at night. A great victory followed for Spain. The shepherd was rewarded by being raised to the nobility. For ever afterward his descendants used either their family name of de Vera or else the honored one of Cabeza de Vaca, which simply meant *cowhead*. Like his ancestors, Alvar Nuñez answered to either name, although de Vaca is the name by which he is known in history.

The Moors were finally driven out of Spain about the time that Alvar was born. He grew up in a gray-walled stone castle, where his father and grandfather, seated by a great fireside on winter nights, discussed endlessly the battles they had fought in their younger years. Such conversations naturally turned young Alvar's mind to thoughts of war. At a time when every adventurous young man who could find a means to reach the New World was doing so, Alvar still remained uninterested in following them.

"I have heard much talk of the wealth of those lands across the Atlantic," he declared to his father. "Not yet, however, have I seen a single Spaniard return to our country with pockets filled with gold. Instead they come with fevers and wounds, and with thin and hungry bodies clad in threadbare garments. Doubtless there are countless others who will never return."

"What will you do if you choose to stay in Spain?" asked his father, the grim, sword-scarred Captain Pedro de Vera. "This countryside is falling into dust and ruin now that there are no longer young men left to shear the sheep and tend the soil. You might fare better to seek your fortune in the New World."

"Until I have been in battle," Alvar replied, "I cannot tell if I would prefer the life of a soldier."

The matter was settled more quickly than Alvar or his father had expected. In the year 1511, when Alvar was eighteen years old, a war began in Italy between the Pope and the Italian princes who ruled their independent states in that country. Alvar Cabeza de Vaca sailed as a junior officer in a Spanish contingent of troops loaned to the Pope by King Ferdinand of Spain.

The two armies met in battle on the plains near the old-world Italian city of Ravenna. For almost the first time in European warfare both sides brought up heavy artillery. The guns—bombards they were usually called—were merely ponderous iron tubes reinforced with tightly bound rope or sometimes oaken staves. But these clumsy-wheeled weapons could hurl murderous charges of iron shot against the closed ranks of an advancing army.

The battle lasted from early morning until nearly sunset. Each army almost destroyed the other. The survivors fled in horror from the bloody slaughter they had caused with cannon fire.

Cabeza de Vaca resigned his commission and went back to Spain. "I could tolerate a war in which men fought with brave weapons," he told his father. "It horrified me to see splendid cavalry blown to bits by some smoke-grimed wretch standing safely behind a bombard several hundred yards away. I will fight no more in the wars of Europe."

Alvar was forced to alter his decision. He had to go to war again, this time in his own country. A rebellion against the Spanish monarchy was started by some of the nobility. Cabeza de Vaca, and his father as well, fought for the cause of the Spanish king. In this war both

[18]

sides still battled mainly with swords, spears, and the ingenious crossbow. Cannon and even the clumsy arquebus—the forerunner of the musket—were regarded as unsporting by both sides.

The civil war lasted for several years. When

it ended, Alvar had come to hate soldiering more than ever. He wanted a quiet and useful life where his love of reading and study of history would find plenty of leisure.

His ambition was satisfied for a few short years. The Spanish king was grateful to the nobility who had fought for his cause in the recent civil war. Young Cabeza de Vaca was rewarded with the governorship of a quiet district. He settled down to his peaceful duties, married a good wife, and surrounded himself with books. But for a chance meeting with a certain man, the name of Alvar Nuñez Cabeza de Vaca might never have figured so brilliantly in the story of the exploration of the New World.

## CHAPTER 2

## *Adventurer in the New World*

IN 1520, when Cabeza de Vaca was already installed as governor and about to be married, fresh exciting news reached Spain. A lean and tireless little Spanish adventurer, accompanied by a couple of hundred mailclad soldiers, had discovered the golden Aztec empire of Mexico.

Hernando Cortes was the name of that Spanish officer. After having led an exciting but spendthrift life, Cortes was now looting the splendid treasures of the emperor Montezuma.

Cabeza de Vaca heard and read the delighted reports of this vast store of gold, emeralds, and silver, which was pouring across the Atlantic and into Spain. The news interested him but aroused neither ambition nor envy in his contented mind. He knew, too, that a Spaniard named Panfilo de Narvaez had once been sent by the jealous governor of Cuba to Mexico with a powerful army. This governor intended to arrest Cortes and take over the conquest of Mexico from him.

Instead, Narvaez was himself taken prisoner by Cortes. He was captured sleeping in his tent, his army was dispersed, and he himself was kicked out of Mexico.

Back in Spain, Narvaez bore a bitter and undying grudge against Cortes. But for that rebellious rascal, he thought constantly, it would have been I who conquered Mexico, thereby gaining for myself fabulous wealth and great honors from the Spanish throne.

For six years Narvaez continued brooding. Jealousy at last put a fresh idea into his head. I will go to discover another Indian country for myself, he decided. I have heard that the unknown country of Florida, so called because it was discovered on *Pascua Florida* (Easter Day) in the year 1513, promises to yield even greater wealth than Cortes seized in Mexico.

It was easy to believe anything one chose about an unexplored country. Narvaez conveniently overlooked the sad history of those who had tried to enter the everglades of Florida, among them Ponce de Leon, whose expedition was wiped out by the Indians.

Thirty-four-year-old Alvar Cabeza de Vaca and Panfilo de Narvaez met in Spain. The Spanish adventurer, soldier, and treasure-seeker was a short, heavy-shouldered man with a sharp-pointed beard, a fierce mustache, the hard features of a successful prison commandant—which he had been in Cuba—and a scarred empty socket where his right eye had once been. He drank enormously, used violent language, and was as obstinate as a bad-tempered mule.

For some strange reason, de Vaca became interested in the idea of exploring Florida. He was certainly not in need of wealth, for both he and his wife were already rich enough. Warfare, particularly one-sided warfare against unfortunate Indians armed with wooden spears instead of swords, did not attract him in the least. To any man accustomed to sleeping in a soft bed and eating three good meals a day, the prospect of marching through subtropical forests and living on salt pork and biscuits would have seemed unpleasant. But de Vaca decided to go to Florida.

"The fabulous city of Cibola must lie somewhere in the interior of that country," declared Panfilo de Narvaez, who was a splendid talker but had no idea of the size of Florida. "Indians

I have tortured declared it is more splendid than any other native kingdom, even than Mexico itself. Why, the very kitchen utensils used by the slaves in the heathen emperor's palace are made of gold. Those Indians said, too, that diamonds as large as these gilt buttons on this coat of mine are used as eyes in life-sized golden statues."

"Such a discovery would be of great value to our young King Charles the Fifth," said de Vaca. "It would be a great service to Spain if we could refill the royal treasure chests by fresh discoveries in Florida."

"Truly it would be a splendid service," de Narvaez replied. He considered it wiser to refrain from saying that he was more interested in his own pockets. De Vaca seemed oddly cool about the prospect of amassing wealth for himself.

"So great a service would it be," de Narvaez continued artfully, "that should you agree to accompany me, I must ask you to act as treasurer for our expedition. The king himself could seek no more honorable person than yourself to safe-guard the royal fifth of the treasure we shall find."

De Narvaez paused for a moment. "Until we find that treasure," he added, "I would also ask you to act as provost-marshal. Spanish troops are inclined to need strong discipline in the tropics. They are easily kept in order with a flogging now and then, or by towing some muti-nous fellow in the sea behind a ship."

Helping de Narvaez to outfit an expedition cost de Vaca most of the money he had saved during his governorship. Between them they raked together five high-decked ships called caravels. Six hundred men—adventurous young aristocrats, officers, and soldiers—somehow found room for themselves on dangerously over-loaded ships, which in modern times would never be allowed by maritime authorities to quit harbor. The fleet sailed from Spain in June, 1527.

In early August the vessels reached the port of San Domingo in the Spanish-owned island of Hispaniola. Partly as a result of a frightening trans-Atlantic voyage, a hundred soldiers promptly deserted. They hid themselves in the forests to avoid recapture and punishment.

"Even with the loss of such useless rascals, we still have many more soldiers than Cortes when he invaded Mexico," declared Narvaez ill-humoredly. "But with five hundred men still to feed, we must sail for Cuba, where I have ways and means to secure cheap fresh provisions for our journey into Florida."

Cabeza de Vaca and another officer sailed along the coast of Cuba in two of the five ships. They were both ashore, buying sackloads of starchy manioc flour in a coastal village, when a hurricane came screaming across the Caribbean Sea. The two anchored vessels were flung onto the beach and smashed to pieces. De Vaca and the few survivors rejoined de Narvaez by land.

"August is undoubtedly the worst hurricane

month of the year," de Narvaez grumbled. "We must keep our remaining three ships in port until spring next year."

"Sire, I beg permission to speak," said a tall Negro named Esteban. He was merely a slave, but during the voyage across the Atlantic Este-

ban had proved he was also a remarkably handy
seaman. After the men had deserted in Hispaniola, he had been promoted to the rank of boat-
swain aboard one of the vessels.

"What is it?" grumbled Narvaez.

"Our ships are unprotected against the borer

worms of these warm seas, my lord Captain-General," Esteban murmured. "Unless we take proper precautions, their timbers will be full of holes next spring."

"A risk all vessels must take in these waters," Narvaez said angrily. "I know it better than you."

"Naturally, sire," replied Esteban, "your highness is wise in all matters. But with your leave I would suggest that we paint the underwater hulls with a mixture of tar and chopped horsehair, after which we nail a thin wood sheathing over the hulls. The borer worms will penetrate this sheathing, but when they come to the horsehair and tar—two substances they dislike greatly —they will seek to drill no further."

"An outlandish and doubtless useless precaution," commented Narvaez, "but I give you leave to try it out. Let the ships be drawn onto the beach at once."

The three vessels were treated in the manner that Esteban recommended. When they were relaunched, their timbers remained almost free of the damage caused by teredos, or marine borers. The Spanish seamen declared with grins that Esteban had brains in his head.

The little fleet sailed for Florida at the beginning of March, 1528. Sickness, death, and more desertions had reduced the numbers on board the three caravels to four hundred men. A great deal of the limited space was taken up by the eighty horses which Narvaez had bought in Cuba. Cavalry was a most valuable weapon against hostile Indians on foot.

From Cuba to the southern end of Florida is a distance of two hundred miles, but Narvaez' ships took six weeks for the voyage. His navigators seem to have been an incompetent lot. They lost all sense of direction in the rainstorms and gales which whipped up the sea. The Caribbean is a shallow sea with short, ugly waves. The luckless vessels tossed up and down with a swift, jerky motion which reduced the soldiers to utter misery from seasickness. Unable to find shelter below deck, they lay huddled in corners, exposed to the wind-driven spray. When fine weather returned, the tropical sunshine reddened and blistered their sea-soaked skins and raised most painful boils on their arms and legs.

On April 12, 1528, the weary little ships sighted a great bay. On either side lay a low, long coastline of shining white sand. Behind it rolled an endless luxuriant jungle. The fleet had reached the natural harbor which later became known as Tampa Bay.

"A fairer prospect than greeted Cortes when he sighted Mexico," declared Narvaez, as he gazed at the distant coast. "His ships came to a sandy desert which lacked water and shade. We shall not go short of either in yonder country."

"Nor perhaps of enemies skillfully concealed in the undergrowth," muttered a dark and wiry little adventurer named Alonso del Castillo. He was one of the few Spanish officers who had survived seasickness, and his weather-tanned skin had successfully resisted the heat of the sun during the voyage from Cuba.

"I recall that when I marched with Balboa to the Pacific Ocean some fourteen years ago," Alonso continued, "it was in the thickest forest that our deadliest enemies always awaited us."

"Captain Balboa had less than two hundred men on that famous expedition," de Vaca replied. "We have double that number."

"And good horses as well," added Narvaez. "You will see, Castillo, that the natives who perhaps lurk in yonder forests will hesitate to attack when they see our cavalry."

The ships dropped anchor within four hundred yards of the silent beach. By nightfall the men were ashore, cooking fires were blazing, and the soldiers, delighted to feel firm ground under their feet, were losing their surly mood.

Next morning they discovered a large native village standing in a clearing. The wooden-walled, palm-thatched huts were empty, but fresh fruit still hung from beams, and cooking

[33]

pots lay abandoned beside the ashes of extinct fires. One of the soldiers discovered a small rattle hidden in an empty gourd on a clumsy shelf. The toy was no longer than a man's forefinger yet the man exclaimed with delight. The rattle was made of gold. The others gathered round to stare at the object and handle it thoughtfully.

"How much gold must there be in this country when Indians can afford to make a child's plaything with such metal!" exclaimed a cavalier named Andres Dorantes. "Surely the great golden city of Cibola cannot lie too far away?"

The first Indians appeared late that afternoon. They came out of the forest and stood on the beach a few hundred yards from the camp. They were tall and finely built men with bronzed skins. Most of them were wearing a waistcloth, but one or two had long glossy cloaks of marten fur which reached well below their knees. Their long hair was coiled in a heavy knot on the top of their well-shaped heads. A narrow plaited band of multicolored cords en-

[34]

circled their foreheads, and from these bands dangled shell ornaments which formed a kind of fringe over their eyes. Across their shoulders were slung tremendous bows, weapons a full six feet in length. One or two of the Indians were holding long and slender spears with sharply barbed points of bone.

The Spaniards gazed thoughtfully at the stalwart figures in the distance. The Indians were pointing to them and thence to the anchored ships. The expressive gestures they made with their hands were enough. They were warning these strangers to return to their vessels and quit the shores of Florida.

"They are taller and more strongly built than the Indians who fought us in Darien," muttered an old soldier named Pozoblanco, who also had marched with Balboa. "Those mighty bows of theirs can doubtless throw a deadly shaft to a great distance. I pray to God their points are not poisoned."

"It is unlikely," said de Vaca, the student of

history. "The men of Ponce de Leon's expedition were oft wounded by arrows in this country, but they did not die of poison."

Cautious old Pozoblanco was not easily comforted. "Perhaps they did not always have time to find out," he said. "For one of those four-foot shafts, driven deeply into a man's body, would quickly cut short his life."

The Indians disappeared into the forest and twilight came. That night there was less singing and laughter in the camp. The men were unusually thoughtful. A number of the crossbowmen were carefully checking their weapons. Perhaps they were wondering how the Spanish crossbow, with its spring laboriously wound back by an iron handle geared to a ratchet, would compare with those mighty, free-shooting longbows carried by the Indians.

The men's doubts and misgivings did not vanish with the return of daylight. That morning de Narvaez called a meeting of all the camp. "Two choices lie open to us," he said. "One is to

[36]

go by land, the other by sea. We can march on foot through the country until we find the glittering city of Cibola, or we can sail along the coast, hoping to sight some splendid province, or perhaps a great highway which will lead us to the city itself. For myself, I prefer to travel by land, even though all the Indians of the Americas should beset my path."

"Your idea is one I welcome, Captain," declared Andres Dorantes, who believed that the city of Cibola was not far away. "The forest is a thousand times better than those accursed ships."

"I would choose to go by sea," Cabeza de Vaca said quietly.

Narvaez stared at him and uttered a short laugh. "Did the ocean so agree with your stomach that you would welcome a return to it?"

De Vaca shook his head. "No, I am guided by what I have read and what I have heard and what I now see around me. In all the Indies the natives have no ships to compare with those of

[37]

Spain. The Aztecs defeated Captain Cortes on land, yet with a few small sailing galleys he at last blockaded their city of Mexico and captured it. In the forest we will be forced to match ourselves man to man against the Indians. They are accustomed to such a battleground, but we are not."

Two other cavaliers, who were veterans of much fighting on land and sea, agreed with Cabeza de Vaca against Andres Dorantes and several others. The argument became hotter as the morning went on. Even the sailors and soldiers were offered a chance to speak. Some of them called on big Esteban to express an opinion.

"My captains and masters, I would travel up the coast of Florida by sea," he said quietly. "Long ago, when I was a mere boy, my own tribe in Africa was at war with the Portuguese. I recall that our chieftain forbade all his warriors to attack the Portuguese in the open. We always awaited them in the forest. Forgive me, my lord, if I dare to speak against your own

[38]

wishes on this matter. I will die readily for you, whether you choose to go by land or sea."

Old Pozoblanco summed up the argument with words of good sense. "It seems, Captain-General," he said to Narvaez, "that those of us who have already fought in bitter wars against the Indians on land would prefer to explore Florida by sea. Our worthy treasurer and provost-marshal, Señor Cabeza de Vaca, agrees with our view. He has wisely let himself be guided by history. It is the young and eager cavaliers, anxious to find gallant adventure on land, who side with your suggestion that we march through this country."

At length the quarrels of the expedition were ended by compromise. After a delay of several weeks it was agreed that the ships would sail north in search of a good harbor. The land party would march in the same direction and at the first great opening in the land they would turn seaward to meet the ships. Narvaez ignored the fact that the expedition was already short of food, and that none could say where the next great bay might lie.

At the head of his cavaliers and fighting men, including Cabeza de Vaca, Narvaez led the way into the treacherous forests of Florida.

# CHAPTER 3

## *A Chieftain's Revenge*

CABEZA DE VACA was seated beside a campfire in the twilight while he wrote in his diary.
The smoke reddened his eyes and they smarted
painfully, but at least it kept off the stinging
mosquitoes. After being a reader of history,
quiet Cabeza de Vaca was now beginning to

write a history that would be read with wonder by future generations.

Today our men seized two Indians, whom we found hidden in a village which we raided in search of corn. Our Captain-General questioned these prisoners by signs, showing them the golden rattle we had found near the coast. They declared with great willingness that northward lies Apalachen, a land in which much gold is to be found. This day, 10 May, 1528, we marched northwestward in the direction of Apalachen.

Apalachen is now the state of Georgia. In pre-European days the Indians of northern Georgia mined gold in small quantities and used it for barter with other tribes.

There was little of the ordinary disciplined march about the Spanish progress up the west coast of Florida. On firm ground they were forced to thrust their way through heavy forests of walnut, oak, mulberry, cherry, and pine. They could seldom walk more than two abreast.

[42]

The thick vegetation so screened the cooling breezes from the sea that the stagnant heat almost choked them. On lower ground they found wide swamps lying across their path. The mud and slime was almost hidden by rank grasses and weeds of a bright and poisonous green. When the Spaniards approached these swamps they found the ground so treacherous that it quivered and shook under their feet for a distance of twenty or thirty feet around.

The horses were terrified. When one boastful young cavalier tried to ride his mount directly into the first swamp, the animal snorted with fright, then reared so violently that his rider was thrown heavily into the soft and evil-smelling mud. He was rescued from suffocation by two men-at-arms, who hauled him out by his heels.

Even worse than the treacherous swamps was the bluish-black, stinking water which lay in their center. Usually this water reached no higher than a man's chest, but there were sudden holes of much greater depth in which the soldiers floundered miserably, for few amongst them knew how to swim.

"Better to die by an Indian arrow than to choke to death in these filthy pits," grumbled Pozoblanco.

He hauled himself onto a massive tree root and proceeded to strip off the heavy cotton-padded jacket which most of the soldiers wore as protection against the native archers. Before long, his example had been followed by all the troops. Only the haughty cavaliers continued to wear the usual long leather jackets over heavy breastplates of shining steel.

At the end of three days' struggling across these dangerous swamps, de Vaca, accompanied by six other veteran officers, formed a deputation to see Narvaez. "We cannot continue in this manner," de Vaca declared frankly. "Nine men and three horses are already dead by drowning, snake bite, or suffocation. The rest grow weary of living, eating, and sleeping in noisome mud or on drier ground where biting insects plague them day and night, and snakes lie under almost every bush."

"Our present journey is even worse than that which we made with Captain Balboa to the Pacific," added dark little Alonso del Castillo. "It will break the hearts and bodies of the men to continue onwards."

Panfilo de Narvaez, who was never an easy-tempered man, had improved neither in mood nor appearance since the march began. His eyes were red from smoke and lack of sleep, and his bearded face was greatly swollen by insect bites. "We cannot turn back," he grumbled. "Our ships have departed from the bay and will be soon awaiting us farther to the north. What purpose would it serve for us to retire to an empty beach?"

"At least we found manioc and corn and coconuts in that district," said one of the men.

"And our men took fish and certain other foods from the sea," added another. "We are already short of food on this march, and there is nothing to eat in this half-drowned and foul-smelling countryside."

"You speak as Cortes' men did when they were crossing the *Tierra Caliente*, the Land of Heat," grumbled Narvaez. "Their stomachs were emptier than our own are now, and where our men die of drowning, they died of cold and starvation in the mountains before they sighted the great city of Mexico, just as we will sight the city of Cibola."

"But first they came to great cultivated fields of corn and fruit, and they ate fowl which they took in the Indian villages," said de Vaca. "This drowned land of mud and forest grows nothing fit for a man to eat."

De Narvaez hesitated for a moment. "Better to die searching for a golden city than waiting to be rescued beside an empty sea," he growled.

"There is a soldier, a man named Arevalo, with us," said de Vaca. "He is greatly skilled in the art of making boats. If we retreated to the

[46]

bay where we landed, he could be set to work to build a craft. Some of us could reach Cuba in it, and there direct other vessels to rescue those who stayed behind. Or, if you wished it, Captain, he could sail in search of our own three vessels which lie somewhere on this coast."

Narvaez, his mind still full of hungry dreams of gold and great fame for himself in Spain, shook his head firmly. "No," he said angrily. "We shall march forward until we find our own golden city or else perish in the effort."

The little Spanish army stumbled and waded northward for another hundred miles. Somewhere near the Suwannee River, the marshes receded temporarily and patches of forest had been cleared for cultivation by tall, brown-skinned Indians. The Spaniards emerged from the trees to see tall fields of corn and manioc and yams growing in the bright sunshine.

The Indians stared with impassive faces. These were the first white men they had seen— these strangers with ragged hair and beards,

[47]

with clothing and armor foul with mud and rust, who scrabbled in the good brown earth for roots which they devoured raw.

The open countryside sloped gently westward to the distant sea. "Perhaps there is a large bay on the coast," suggested Narvaez. "We will send a party of men to look for the ships."

The scouts were gone for four days. They returned with gloomy faces.

"They saw no sign of vessels," wrote de Vaca in his diary. "They declared that great forests stretched down to the coast so that no man could see further than the next headland. When our men questioned the Indians they met, the natives said that they had seen no ship along that part of the coast."

The Suwannee Indians remained good-natured despite their looted fields. For several days they fed the Spaniards with fish and eels, platters of cooked vegetables and deer meat. But Narvaez' men did not behave in a grateful manner. The soldiers turned the Indians out of their huts and took them for their own use. They helped themselves freely to every pot of food, and ransacked the village in search of gold.

"These people will turn against us if we continue to handle them so roughly," warned Alonso del Castillo. "It was a matter in which Captain Balboa was always careful to restrain his men."

His words were ignored by Narvaez and most of the Spanish officers. Soon the Indians vanished into the forest. As the Spaniards loitered in the village and scanned their few reserves of food, a cloud of arrows came whistling down from the sky. One cavalier died with a shaft through his chest, and three soldiers were killed. Amongst them was Arevalo, the soldier who alone understood the craft of boat building.

"We march northwards," Narvaez said grimly. "Whatever it may cost, we must reach our ships."

They took to the trackless forests again, still heading northwestward in search of golden Apalachen. Instead of gold they found fresh swamps. Sickness and death came to them from fever, snake bite, and drowning. Narvaez was growing frenzied in his quest for gold. Eight weeks after he had landed in Florida he was torturing nearly every Indian his men captured in an attempt to find information regarding Apalachen, or Cibola, or whatever city his half-crazy mind believed held the gold he craved.

At last the day came when two Indians, whose screams had rung loudly through the green twilight of the forest, uttered frenzied words which delighted Narvaez.

These two miserable beings said that Golden Apalachen lay but two days' journey to the northward. They gave other information about it which gratified our Captain-General, but he ordered the two prisoners to be detained until we have proved the truth, or otherwise, of their story.

Lean, mud-stained Cabeza de Vaca was developing an instinct for caution which amounted almost to disbelief of every Indian report. His thoughtful face was shadowed by doubt as he wrote the phrase "the truth, or otherwise," on a damp page of his diary. He did not believe that the truth could be ascertained from Indians by burning the soles of their feet with iron ramrods. Had he been free to choose, he would have adopted kinder, more Christian, methods. But de Vaca's mind was three centuries ahead of European thought in that age. His countrymen regarded all heathen merely as animals; he took them to be human beings much like himself or any other man. For that reason a kindly friendship had already grown up between himself and big Esteban, the African Negro.

"Apalachen lies but two days' journey ahead," ran the crazy rumor through the Spanish ranks. "There is gold in plenty for every man amongst us."

The men scrambled onward through foul-smelling morasses of mud and stagnant water,

with big brown leeches clinging to their hands
and faces. Many of the men were so ill with
fever that they looked like unshaven ghosts as
they staggered along. Forty-one horses out of
the original eighty were still alive, and three
hundred and forty men out of the four hundred

who had landed at Tampa still marched behind
Narvaez.

They sighted Apalachen at daybreak on the
third day. It was no great white-walled city
like Mexico, fairer than any in Europe, arising
from the placid waters of a shining lake. It was

merely a scattered collection of perhaps sixty mud-walled huts with thickly thatched roofs. Certainly there was a lake nearby—probably Lake Miccosukee in modern Jefferson County. On its surface nothing floated except a flock of wild ducks and a derelict fishing canoe.

So firmly had the Spaniards believed the story of Apalachen's golden treasure that even now they could not realize that this primitive Indian village in a grassy clearing was merely what it appeared. Hunger and sickness, heat and gold fever, had affected their brains.

> Our cavalry attacked this town in a great charge and the soldiers advanced swiftly on it under my command. We met with no resistance, a matter which was scarce surprising for the only inhabitants were women and children; the menfolk, it appeared, being absent on some errand of their own. Our men looted and plunged amongst the huts and drove out the women and children, yet we found no gold nor other treasure.

At least the Spaniards found something that

was more useful to them in their starving condition. The land around the village was carefully tilled and planted with crops. The thickly wooded country was filled with deer, and great numbers of small but edible fish swam in the lake. In their usual highhanded manner the soldiers set the women and children to pounding corn, gathering yams from the fields, washing clothes, and cooking meals. Only a few of the more thoughtful cavaliers, including impetuous Andres Dorantes, became alarmed by the situation in which they found themselves.

"I have seen native women enslaved in Cuba and Hispaniola," he said. "They were poor, timorous creatures, hastening to obey the least command of their masters. But there is a strange resolution about these hardy Indian women of Apalachen. They obey us, but they are not afraid of us. Some secret thought is keeping their courage high. I wish I knew what it is."

Dorantes and his companions found the answer two weeks after they arrived at Apalachen.

The chief of that region was a fearsome chief named Hirrihigua, a man well over six feet in height, gifted with cunning powers as a leader. He was as cruel and malevolent as a jungle cat and he possessed much of that animal's ferocity. Apalachen was the village where he dwelt. His wife and children were being compelled to work as slaves for harsh, ill-tempered Spanish soldiery.

This news was brought to Hirrihigua by a boy who had fled into the forest when the Spaniards attacked the village. Instinct warned Hirrihigua not to attack the Spaniards in battle. Horses were a novelty to him, and he was shrewd enough to guess—or perhaps some spy told him—that these animals could be used as a powerful weapon against an enemy on foot in the open. He and his warriors remained in the forest, crouching low in the undergrowth with their bows constantly in hand. From morning to night they kept watch on the village.

Five Spanish soldiers were cutting long grass

for the horses in Apalachen when death came to them out of the forest. They were pierced from chest to backbone, through leather jacket and shirt. The bodies were left where they lay with great four-foot shafts protruding from them. Every one of the five unfortunate soldiers was scalped. Four others were killed when they ventured outside the village.

The alarmed Spaniards began keeping close to the protecting walls of the huts. This was a new and terrible kind of warfare to them. No noisy crash of firearms accompanied it, no roll of drum or note of fife. No standards waved in the breeze, no splendid charge of mailclad cavaliers with steel-tipped lances took place. The Spaniards crawled and dodged from wall to wall and hut to hut like hunted animals. At any moment that terrible noiseless death might reach swiftly out to them from the cool green forest.

Not even the hard-faced Narvaez and the veteran officers who formed his council cared to remain any longer in Apalachen. The swamps and the trackless forests seemed better than this prosperous village. For perhaps the first time in their lives the Spaniards were confronted by an enemy more cunning than themselves and of appalling tenacity.

For three weeks the Spaniards endured Apalachen; then with a haste that was almost panic, they fled from the place.

> We traveled south in quest of a rumored village named Aute. This place was said to be on the seacoast, and although it lacked gold, our Captain-General had heard the agreeable tidings that there was an abundance of natural foods in the region.

This was almost the last occasion on which de Vaca mentioned gold in his diary. From the day the expedition had first landed in Florida he had remained cool and doubtful about the rumored wealth of the country. His companions might still be filled with gold fever in spite of their sufferings, but Cabeza de Vaca had realized for some time past that a fertile countryside would be more likely to save their lives.

Hirrihigua still showed his cold hatred of the invaders after they had vacated his village. Most chieftains would have withdrawn to celebrate the victory and left the enemy to escape any way they could. Hirrihigua and his tall warriors went on stalking the Spaniards through the forest. Now that the trees made the use of cavalry impossible, the Indians started attacking at fords and lake crossings. These great, gaunt, painted warriors wielded terrible bows, compared with which the slow-firing Spanish crossbow was an ingenious toy. Steel helmets and plate armor split under the impact of arrowheads hardened in fire and water. When the fighting came to close quarters, the Indians often swung their massive oak bows with astounding strength and skill, using them as deadly clubs.

Old Pozoblanco disappeared into a swamp, grappling with the Indian warrior who had tackled him. Two others who had warned Narvaez against the overland march were severely wounded. Cabeza de Vaca was struck in the shoulder by an arrow which penetrated to his collarbone and had to be cut out with a knife.

The expedition continued to struggle desperately onward through the hot damp forests to the seacoast. Behind them they left a growing number of graves.

On the fourteenth day after leaving the village of Apalachen, the south wind brought a cool and salty flavor to the stagnant, damp-filled air of the forest. That evening the Spaniards emerged from the bush and saw in front of them an open but rocky stretch of country. In the center of it rose crumbled walls of mud and the skeletons of charred roofs from which smoke was still rising. This was Aute village. The Indians had set fire to the place before escaping.

"We must go forward to the sea," Narvaez ordered de Vaca. "Our ships must be anchored somewhere nearby. Take what men you need for the journey. I will remain here and build a camp in which our sick and wounded may have some chance to recover."

De Vaca went with forty soldiers, as great a

number as the sick and crumbling Spanish expedition could spare.

We found the country to be very rough and craggy, covered with forests, swamps, rivers, and troublesome passages. It was poorly populated and sterile. Although the Indians nearly always left us alone, the hardships of our journey to the coast were very considerable. Being short of food we ate whatever we could find on the way, including a kind of yam and half-ripe corn which we boiled.

De Vaca reached the coast at last. Somewhere on the shores of Apalachee Bay he paused to gaze out across an empty sea with eyes which now held little expression of hope. The ships had not come.

After searching vainly for Narvaez along the coast, the vessels had finally returned to Cuba, believing that his expedition had been wiped out.

A few miles inland, the exhausted army which depended on them was crumbling swiftly into ruins.

# CHAPTER 4

## *The Amateur Boatbuilders*

NARVAEZ and his men were encamped on a patch of open and barren ground no more than a mile in length and about half that in width. Around the limits of this clearing rose the tall fringe of the forest. The undergrowth was so dense that although crisscrossed with meandering tracks made by wolves, bear, deer, and opossums, anyone who stepped aside into this damp green foliage of leaf and fern was immediately lost to sight. Hidden amongst the trees, Hirrihigua and his tireless warriors awaited a chance to destroy the strangers' camp.

Narvaez and perhaps a dozen of his officers owned small circular tents. The rest of the men slept and ate in tiny huts, which they made for themselves, using sticks as a framework over which they spread cloaks and saddleblankets. These hovels provided shade from the midday heat, but they gave little protection against heavy rain, and none at all against myriads of mosquitoes and black flies.

After Cabeza and his company returned to this camp, Castillo remarked with a grin, "Were I to find one of my cherished horses in Cuba housed in such a miserable hovel as the one I now occupy, I would have the slave responsible thrashed most soundly."

Four days had passed since Cabeza de Vaca

and his men had come back with the depressing news that they found no trace of the ships. Alone in his tent, a grim-faced Narvaez was considering what to do next. He would gain nothing by retreating through the filthy swamps to Tampa Bay, which now lay a good three hundred miles to the south. Nor could he go forward in further desperate search of golden cities. He had lost too many men already; only two hundred and fifty of the original four hundred who had landed from the ships were still alive. At least half of them were too weak from wounds, sickness, hunger, or a combination of all three, to sustain many more marches across this wild and hostile country. Yet to remain where they were, encamped on this inhospitable open ground, meant awaiting death by starvation or tomahawks.

It was Hirrihigua who caused Narvaez to reach a decision. Late at night the Indians came creeping out of the woods, armed with lance, tomahawk, and scalping knife. They crawled to within a few yards of the camp before a tired but suspicious sentry noticed the gliding figures in the firelight. He was killed as he shouted an alarm, but the sudden barking of the Spanish boarhounds, of which there were about a dozen in the camp, aroused the men. Many of them were still buckling on steel breastplates or fumbling for crossbow and lance and sword when the Indians were on them. Tall, almost naked figures, with painted faces, came bounding out of the forest, swinging tomahawks and darting slender spears.

Several Spaniards died before they were properly awake. Others were struck down by unseen attackers while their sleepy eyes were still struggling to grow accustomed to the darkness. There was no time to form any continuous line of defense. The Spaniards formed into little groups and fought where they stood. They were unable to hear any orders shouted by their officers. The Indians were screaming and whooping as they hacked and thrust, and the great boarhounds were snarling loudly as they slashed with terrible fangs at the warriors.

The attack lasted from eleven o'clock at night until dawn was showing in the sky. The Indians then retreated swiftly to the forest. They had lost at least thirty warriors during the fight. At close quarters, the European sword and lance, steel armor and helmet, gave the Spaniards some advantage. Officers and soldiers alike were skilled hand-to-hand fighters; they dreaded the tomahawk and lance much less than those terrible longbows. Even so, eighteen Spaniards died during that bitter fight. Another twenty were wounded.

While the men washed their sweating bodies in cold water from a nearby spring, and boiled their miserable breakfast of horseflesh mixed with grass and tender bark stripped from bushes, Narvaez called a conference of his officers.

"Last night's work has shown us that we can no longer travel by land," he declared. "Henceforth we must take to the sea."

Andres Dorantes smiled harshly. He wore a bloodstained cloth round his head, for he had narrowly missed death from a thrown tomahawk. "So the ocean wins at last, Captain-General! When we first discussed whether we should go by land or sea, I spoke in favor of the land. I am here this morning, but many of those who shared my opinion are no longer present. My honor prompts me to declare frankly that my decision was a wrong one. I trust the Captain-General will take no offense."

"By the words I have already spoken this morning, I confessed my own mistake," Narvaez said bluntly. "We should have explored this deadly coast by sea. It is not too late to do so now."

"A matter on which there may be some doubt, Captain," snapped Alonso del Castillo. He was one of those who had declared hotly against proceeding by land. "Our only boatbuilder, the soldier called Arevalo, is dead. Which man amongst us has any knowledge of the craft in which he was skilled?"

"The matter will be raised forthwith amongst the troops," Narvaez said wearily. "Possibly a few of them may know at least something of carpentry."

De Vaca asked the next question. "Provided we build some vessels, Captain, whither will we sail?"

"To Tampico in Mexico," Narvaez replied. "It is the most northerly of our Spanish settlements in that country. If we sail westward far enough along this infernal coast, we must come to Tampico at last. We dare not risk crossing the open seas to Cuba. We lack all of the instruments that mariners use, and our boats—when we build them—will be too frail for such a voyage."

Cabeza de Vaca opened his diary that evening in the blanket-covered hovel he occupied. Slowly and carefully, choosing his words with scholarly precision, he wrote:

Our Captain-General has decided to march southward in the direction of the sea. It is his opinion that if all trace of our ships be lacking, we shall build a number of barges by means of which, and while continuing in sight of land, we may come at last to the province of Tampico. Doubtless our voyage will be fraught with many dangers, for our supplies of victuals are woefully short and many of our men are sick or wounded.

The Spaniards marched out of their camp toward the sea. They no longer resembled a well-disciplined and resolute exploring expedition. The weakest or more seriously wounded men rode on the backs of the twenty-seven remaining horses. Others were carried on rough litters made of blankets and freshly cut poles. The once burnished armor was now rusty and dented by many a blow; the men's clothing frayed and gaping with rents. Shoes were merely shapeless and pulpy lumps of leather, bound to the feet with knotted cords. Men's hair and beards were long and ragged and unkempt, and trimmed only with a knife when their length became inconvenient. But because they were still soldiers of Spain, and possessed of great courage and pride in their country, every man's sword or lance, arquebus or cross-bow, was still bright and clean and ready for fresh battle. The Spaniards were prepared to fight on until the last of them was dead.

Hirrihigua, that vengeful and determined chief, would still not let the Spaniards depart quietly from the country to seek safety as best they could. His warriors continued to harass the invaders by day and night. The Indians had now realized that their longbows were the best weapon; they risked no more hand-to-hand bat-tles. They concealed themselves in the forest beside rivers and swamps and rocky defiles— anywhere, in fact, that the Spaniards were forced to travel slowly or even make a halt. The twanging deerskin cords continued to send those terrible flying shafts to cause fresh wounds and deaths amongst the retreating enemy.

At one river crossing a lucky shot from an arquebus killed an Indian warrior who was taking cover behind a rock. Two of the cavaliers rode out and recovered the man's bow and arrows. Time after time the Spaniards had seen the Indians pull back the cord of these weapons until it was level with their cheeks. They achieved this feat apparently without difficulty. Yet when one strong young cavalier attempted to do the same, he could do no more than pull the string halfway back to his own cheek. None of the other Spaniards who handled the weapon could even do as much.

Alonso del Castillo, who had been watching these efforts, quietly unbuckled his steel hauberk, the fine breastplate which covered his chest, and flung it contemptuously into the river. "It cost me a hundred and fifty ducats in Spain," he jested. "The armorer who made it for me declared the thing was proof against the bolt of any crossbow in Europe. But now that I have seen close at hand the strength of an Indian bow, I place no more faith in mail. Many of those who did are already dead. From now on

[71]

I will wear the cheap cotton-padded tunic used by our soldiers. It is lighter and cooler, and it may help to preserve my life better than that sheet of iron."

The Spaniards reached the coast on the third day. They camped beside the beach of wide and spacious Apalachee Bay. A nearby stream provided them with all the drinking water they needed. The sandy, open country gave some protection against the lurking warriors. Apart from these two advantages, there was little else to be grateful for.

Esteban, the African Negro, knew enough about ships to plan the length and breadth of the proposed barges. He knew how the ribs should be curved and the planks fastened to them. He could also advise on the stepping of masts and the fitting of sails. "But I have no skill with European tools, sire," he told the gloomy Narvaez. "I can merely sail a ship built by hands more capable than mine."

"I doubt if the most skilled artisan in Spain could build a proper vessel with what tools we have," de Vaca interjected drily. "We came to this country as soldiers and explorers, not as shipwrights."

Amongst some two hundred and fifteen Spaniards there were sadly few trained in any useful trade. On Esteban and three others Narvaez had to rely for the boats in which to escape. When it came to tools, the Captain-General found himself rather better provided.

There were four long crosscut saws which had been intended for the building of huts or a fort. On the other hand, only two small handsaws could be found. Axes were somewhat more numerous, seven or eight of different sizes being available. The farrier was able to supply a number of hammers and also a great many new horseshoes which would come in useful for the making of iron bolts. This farrier was a reasonably skilled man at iron work. He was given the task of preparing the bolts.

There were no chisels, planes, or drills, and only two long-handled adzes.

Such was the limited equipment with which

Narvaez ordered the building of five barges, each capable of holding about forty men. Fortunately, a large grove of oak and walnut and pine trees grew within two hundred yards of the camp. At least there would be no shortage of excellent timber.

For thirty days the Spaniards worked from dawn to dusk. No distinction was made between aristocratic gentleman and humble soldier. Every man was given his special task for the day, and all had to take a hand in the heavy work of sawing planks from the trunks of fallen trees. This was a particularly dangerous task as the fringe of the main forest was within arrow shot of the site. Hirrihigua and his warriors appeared at last to have returned to their own country, but the local Indians were always awaiting a chance to kill some Spaniard. A strong guard of soldiers had to remain with the workers, while the latter wearily heaved the saws back and forth.

Cavaliers who had never handled a tool in their lives learned how to swing an ax or wield a hammer. They carried planks and drove in iron spikes. Alonso del Castillo, a fine horseman and expert swordsman, was given the task of collecting resin from the pine trees with which to fill the chinks between the planks. De Vaca, the former state governor and classical scholar, now helped the farrier in changing red-hot horseshoes into eight-inch nails. Andres Dorantes, a born gentleman adventurer, found himself placed in charge of the sick and wounded, whom he was forced to tend daily with his own hands.

On the other hand, Esteban became a man of some authority. He alone knew something of the theory of shipbuilding, and his practical familiarity with vessels helped to guide him in advising how the planks should be secured to the ribs, or the keel laid for a new barge.

The first boat was launched from the beach. It was a great hulk some twenty-six feet in length, eight feet in beam, and two feet in draft. Yet the thing floated on a reasonably even keel, somewhat to the surprise of the men who had

toiled and sweated to build it. They hauled it
out of the water again, fearing that a rough sea
might wreck the clumsy barge. Considerably
encouraged, they hastened to complete the con-
struction of the remaining four boats. Meanwhile, a number of men began killing off the

horses and curing the flesh over smoky fires. The skins they used to make clumsy water bags. Other parties ventured into the woods to collect wild plums and grapes, which they dried in the sun, and also nuts and acorns.

The voyage began in January, 1529. One by

one the five barges were pulled out to sea by men freshly learning how to swing the long and clumsy sweeps, which would soon blister their hands. Each boat was fitted with a short mast from which hung a patchwork sail made of blankets, shirts, and other garments.

"The prevailing winds seem to blow toward the west," Esteban suggested to Narvaez. "If we can use their force, sire, our voyage may be made more speedily. The oars will only be necessary when the breeze drops."

The sails were now hoisted on the bamboo yards. Sluggishly the barges swung westward as inexpert helmsmen discovered how the steering oars should be manipulated. The white shore receded into the distance, and from the green forest there appeared groups of Indians who stood gazing after the boats from the water's edge.

Beneath a tropic sun, across a calm ocean of dazzling blue, Narvaez' little fleet set forth on its desperate voyage to distant Tampico.

## CHAPTER 5

*The Desperate Voyage*

DE VACA huddled in the tiny patch of shade afforded by the tattered awning above his head. The screen was made from his one remaining shirt and a tattered fragment of blanket. It was supported by lines which ran across the boat, from one side to the other. The lines themselves were leather reins, but the horse he had once guided with them was dead.

Days of hot sunshine and burning winds had blackened de Vaca's skin. His dark, unkempt hair reached almost to his shoulders. His once neatly trimmed black beard was long and tangled and caked with salt. There was nothing about his appearance to distinguish him from the forty-one men huddled together in this barge he now commanded. But de Vaca was still keeping a reasonably accurate record of the voyage.

Reaching into a stained saddlebag, he drew out his leather-bound diary, which for further protection against the elements was wrapped in a goatskin bag, a quill made from the wing of a wild turkey, and a bottle of ink composed of vegetable juices.

We have now passed five days at sea, during

[80]

which time we have voyaged perhaps seventy leagues (210 miles) to the westward. We do not dare to lose sight of the land for fear of committing ourselves to an empty ocean. Of the four other barges, all remain in sight and at a distance of not more than a league from ourselves. We continue to sail under the united command of our Captain-General.

The hardships and misfortunes of the past ten months had at last taught Narvaez to be cautious. The low and sandy coast was mostly barren, but wherever a patch of greenery gave promise of water and edible vegetables, he ordered the boats ashore to find whatever supplies they could. The cured horseflesh and dried fruits, he insisted, should be spared as much as possible.

The Spaniards' greatest problem was water. The leather drinking bags leaked badly. When filled they contained sufficient water for only five days. On the day that de Vaca noted in his diary that the barges had sailed two hundred

and ten miles, the water was almost finished. Another two days of thirst under a blazing sun were to be endured before the leading vessel, in which Esteban was acting as sailing master, sighted the deep and sprawling entrance to Pensacola Bay.

As soon as the barges grounded on the yellow sand at the landward end of this inlet, the Spaniards leaped overside into the warm surf. A

hundred yards away they could see a deep and narrow stream flowing to the sea between banks covered with grass and flowers. Careless of weapons, scarcely pausing to help ashore those comrades who were too weak to walk, they ran desperately to the creek and plunged their burning bodies into the water.

"Drink prudently," called Alonso del Castillo. "I have seen thirst-tortured men die because they overfilled their stomachs with water when they came to a spring."

Other Spanish officers took up the warning cry, but their voices were weak and passed unheard. Even the shaggy, sun-blackened Narvaez was ignored as the soldiers flung themselves into the cool water.

A quarter of an hour later, many of the Spaniards were rolling on the ground in agony from stomach cramps. Four of them died before evening. They were buried at dawn the following morning beside two companions whose bodies had been brought ashore from the barges.

A wandering party of dark-skinned Indians stared at the six wooden crosses and then at the ragged and haggard men sprawling in the shade of some trees. They spoke amongst themselves for a while, then went away. They returned in the afternoon. With them they brought baskets of cooked beans, two young deer, a turkey, and a large gourd containing a hash made of fish and corn.

The Spaniards no longer took these things as haughty conquerors. Veteran soldiers wept with gratitude as they received their share of food. The soldier who had discovered the rattle seemed as overjoyed at receiving a deer's shinbone as an extra titbit as he had been over the golden toy. Narvaez himself, who had seldom been known to show any humanity to an Indian, presented the leader of these nomadic hunters with a fine dagger, a silver necklace, and three iron spikes.

The Indians stood on the beach to watch the Spaniards wading back to their barges. The vessels were already hoisting their sails when one of the men leaped into the sea and joined the Indians.

"We must start rowing," shouted Narvaez across the water, but de Vaca stood up to call back an alternative suggestion.

"This is the first day on which the wind has not blown steadily," he said. "Rowing will weary our sick and exhausted men, and increase their craving for water. We would do better, Captain-General, to await the return of the breeze. Should it not come soon, then we can return to the bay of the Indians. If we continue to move westward, we may search for many days before finding another convenient place to land."

For thirty-six hours the boats rose and fell gently on the uneasy surface of the Gulf. Toward evening a light breeze came from the east. By nightfall the barges were lumbering along under the pull of their patched and crazy sails.

This was not the first occasion on which de Vaca had made some suggestion regarding the navigation of the barges. Narvaez was a strong and self-confident leader on land, but the sea was a strange element to him. He lacked the quick ability to learn its moods, which apparently de Vaca possessed. From then on Narvaez began to seek de Vaca's opinion more often. At times he even listened to the humble suggestions made by Esteban. The Negro had already proved the best sailing master in the barges, for his own craft was always in the lead whatever the state of the weather.

A hundred miles to the westward, and just as the water bags became empty again, de Vaca's barge sighted Mobile Bay. The boats came to rest beside a low promontory, on which stood a large Indian village.

A couple of shallow streams flowed into the nearby sea. The Spaniards, having learned caution now, and also being less thirsty than on the last occasion, quenched their thirst more prudently.

The Indians gazed in wonder at these wild-looking strangers from the sea. Soon they began bringing corn and fish, bear's meat, and large pumpkins to the beach. After the Spaniards had again filled their stomachs with these ample supplies of food, the Indians pointed to the village and made signs that the visitors should sleep there.

"Sometimes the Aztecs used that same trick

in an attempt to destroy Cortes," said Narvaez. "We will not go with them to yonder village."

"A wise precaution, Captain," agreed Castillo. "Twice I have all but lost my life because I accepted Indian hospitality. A watchful boarhound saved me on one occasion and my own instincts on the other."

The Indians were gigantic men, larger even than the Seminoles in the forests to the north of Tampa Bay. Probably they belonged to the Creek tribe, who were once famous for their size, intelligence, and artistic skills. De Vaca was greatly impressed by them.

The greater number of these natives were dressed in very fine fur cloaks and a serviceable white cloth of some sort. They had many colored beads and other small trinkets which they used in great numbers to hang upon their necks, and ornament their moccasins and beautiful belts. Their appearance was of great dignity and manliness.

That night the Spaniards rolled themselves in

their blankets to sleep on the beach, while a number of others remained on board the barges.

Discipline was breaking down amongst them. Narvaez had given the strictest orders that no Spaniard was to enter the village on any excuse whatsoever. Two foolish soldiers, in search perhaps of strong liquor or gold, disobeyed this command. They were seen and challenged by some Indian in a dark lane between the huts. He yelled an alarm and they stabbed him to death.

The warriors killed the two soldiers before they had a chance to escape. Then, enraged by the murder, they ran down the easy slope of the hillside and fell upon the Spanish camp.

Narvaez had chosen to sleep in one of the barges. De Vaca was the senior officer ashore. As the Spanish trumpets shrilled an alarm, he tried to organize a defense. The Indians were upon them before the Spaniards were properly awake, and the war party charged right through the camp.

[89]

As the Creeks turned to make another charge, the soldiers formed into a rough line to resist them. From then until dawn a bloody fight raged between scattered and smoldering camp-fires, overturned cooking pots, and prostrate bodies.

When daylight came the arquebusiers opened slow and clumsy fire with their ponderous weapons. The Indians, astonished by the smoke and thunderous discharge of these firearms, drew off hastily and returned to their village.

Narvaez came ashore to view the scene of the fight. He was in a bitter and revengeful mood. "We must teach these traitorous savages a lesson," he growled. "We will march to their village and destroy every living person in it."

"We would do better to leave them alone," one officer said in an ill-humored voice. "Fifteen of our men lie dead yonder, and at least the same number lie grievously wounded. How many more lives would it cost to burn the Indians out of their village?"

Narvaez glanced at the grimed and haggard faces around him. They indicated the truth in a surly manner. These men of his were sick of fighting and anxious only to continue their desperate voyage. Not one of them was eager to risk his life in a battle fought merely for the sake of revenge.

"Perhaps," one man suggested quietly, "the Captain-General would be content with destroying yonder canoes on the beach. It would serve as a sharp punishment."

Narvaez relaxed and his angry expression faded. "Yes," he said. "Order the canoes to be destroyed. When the task is finished, we will sail at once."

Ax-swinging soldiers chopped to pieces thirty large and handsome canoes. Meanwhile, the dead Spaniards were buried in the sandy turf above the beach, and the whole expedition returned to the barges. Once again they sailed onward to the west, past the long, creaming weariness of surf which marked the shore line.

## CHAPTER 6

### *The Coast of Texas*

CABEZA DE VACA was rapidly moving into
the position of leader amongst the men. His
barge now kept abreast of Esteban's throughout
the long and sweltering days, for he had learned
rapidly how to make the most of wind and sea.
His thoughtful mind had studied weather signs,

and he had developed a gift for picking out spots on the coast where fresh water and growing foodstuffs could be used to revictual the fleet. Thirty days at sea had caused him to change from a quiet and cultured gentleman to a ragged, hardy, and competent seaman. Noticing and approving of this change, his companions now paid more attention to his opinions and asked him often for advice.

The vessel in which I sailed being in advance of the others at the time, we were the first to sight what I took to be the mouth of some very large river. The water through which we sailed became brown as if charged with mud, and when we drew up a pail of it, we wondered greatly to discover that it was fresh water which could be drunk without harm. The current in this region was most turbulent and our boats were buffeted by it to an alarming extent. Indeed, the outflow of this great volume of water into the sea caused us to be carried southward until we lost sight of the land.

De Vaca was the first European to note the

existence of the Mississippi River. He and his companions were also the first to be borne on its waters where they blended with the sea.

It was a terrifying experience for the Spaniards. They found themselves drifting across the wide and empty waters of the Gulf of Mexico, short of provisions and with rapidly emptying water bags. The current, which had borne them hither so treacherously, disappeared, and the breeze was so light that the barges traveled at a mere two miles an hour.

It was Esteban, the one man who knew the stars, who kept the boats working up toward the northwest again throughout the hot damp nights. During the day, the position of the sun served as a rough guide. By this time the men were living on a small handful of food and a single cup of water as their daily ration. They dropped exhausted through heat, malaria, thirst, and hunger.

Esteban brought the vessels in sight of land eight days after the Mississippi had swept them out to sea, and they crawled ashore on a low flat coast in the dawn. For six days they camped beside a single spring from which bubbled strangely bitter water. For food they grubbed up plantains, sought for shellfish amongst the rocks, and killed their last surviving dog.

A band of Indians appeared on the fourth day. They were a lean and hungry-looking crowd, friendly enough but without any food to give away except a single bag of pemmican— bear's meat dried, pounded, and pressed into greasy cakes. These Indians remained in the vicinity only one night. Next morning they were gone, and with them went a Negro slave belonging to Narvaez and a Greek foot soldier. These two men preferred life with the Indians to their unending terror of the sea.

Yet perhaps this voyage had gone better up to the present than some of the Spaniards expected. The clumsy, ill-equipped barges had managed to remain afloat during a voyage which had already covered six hundred miles, from Apalachee Bay to the vicinity of Marsh Island in Louisiana. They had, indeed, already accomplished more than one third of the distance to Tampico in Mexico.

After spending a week ashore, the men had recovered some of their strength. They refilled the water bags, carried aboard the barges whatever supplies of food they could gather, and sailed again.

That night the breeze dropped suddenly. De Vaca, whose barge was in the lead, saw with horror that the glow of distant campfires along the coast was again fading from sight. Another mysterious current was forcing his boat away from land.

"Out oars," he ordered. "We must row until we are past this stream and near to the coast again."

Throughout the night the forty Spaniards on board took turns pulling the eight long and ponderous sweeps. But the current was more powerful than their own feeble efforts. When morning returned, the land was lost to view. Only one other barge remained in sight, the one sailed by Esteban.

De Vaca held a conversation with this other barge across the calm sea. The crew had also rowed all night. Like de Vaca's men they were now drooping with exhaustion.

"Let us rest throughout the day," suggested one soldier. "While the wind refuses to blow and the current sweeps us southward, we can only commend our souls to God. It is what Esteban advises."

The long, hot, and windless day passed slowly. Toward evening the weary, sun-blistered men began to stir from under their primitive awnings. They were each served with a handful of corn, a spoonful of pemmican, and a cup of water.

An hour later Esteban called across the water. "Señor de Vaca, the current has ceased to thrust us south. We can make progress to the northwest now, back to the coast we have left."

"Our men rowed for the space of about two hours," de Vaca wrote, "and then a wind from the east filled our sail so generously that the rotten material of which it was made threatened

to split. Heavy rain fell toward midnight. We spread out cloths in which to catch this gift of God and then squeezed the cloths into our water bags. By this means we were able to replenish our stocks of water and every man was able to satisfy his own exceeding thirst."

During the seven days that followed, de Vaca and those with him learned how to fight to keep a ship alive. A chilly wet gale whipped the sea into the high waves of the shallow Caribbean Sea. They rode out this storm by means of a floating anchor made of odd pieces of timber which kept the vessel's bow pointing into the wind. Men bailed with helmets, bowls, and any other receptacle they could find. Their remaining stocks of food became soggy and unpleasant masses of pulp in moldering leather bags, but the frightful motion of the vessel so weakened them with seasickness that few Spaniards felt any great hunger.

At last the wind slackened off slightly. De Vaca saw the men in Esteban's barge haul in the sea anchor and prepare to run before the gale. He followed this example. For two days and nights the vessels plunged onward to the northwest.

Disaster ended this last wild race across the foam-streaked sea. Esteban, that alert and careful seaman, lay deep in exhausted slumber at the time. Both sea and wind were going down and the barges were riding more easily than they had during the past week. The Negro probably believed that all danger was past.

In the middle of the night I was awakened to hear the tumbling of the sea; for as the coast was low it roared loudly. Before we could turn away from the land, a wave flung our vessels amongst the rocks. By God's mercy I survived this great danger and crawled onto the beach, where we could do naught except endure the great cold while we waited for the coming of the dawn.

In the cheerless gray light of early morning, de Vaca found himself on a forlorn and empty shore, between a line of sand hills and the sea. Lying by the water's edge were the bodies of the men who had sailed so long and courageously with him.

Only three men had survived. They were Alonso del Castillo, the veteran who had marched with Balboa; Andres Dorantes, the young and ambitious cavalier; and Esteban, the tall and wiry Negro.

## CHAPTER 7

### *Life with the Comanche Indians*

DE VACA was on the beach of an island near the bay where the city of Galveston, Texas, would one day stand. Seven hundred miles to the east lay Apalachee Bay, where the voyage had begun. Six hundred miles to the southwest was Tampico. The date was the middle of April in the year 1529. De Vaca had been in North America for a year and, with his surviving companions, had seen more of the continent than any other man alive. But his travels were not yet ended; indeed, the most extraordinary of them had not yet begun.

A band of Indians appeared on the beach while de Vaca and the others were still gratefully warming their chilled bodies in the growing heat of the sun. Smiling and patting the shipwrecked men on the cheeks and shoulders, the natives guided them to a small village of a dozen tents. Here the Spaniards were invited by signs to strip off their wet and ragged clothing and dress themselves in comfortable leggings of dressed skins, a breech clout of the same material, very beautifully ornamented with shells, and long, light fur cloaks.

Dorantes, a somewhat haughty young man, refused to make the change. He could not accustom himself yet to the idea that he was living amongst savages whom he had learned to hate, and that he was to be fed and clothed by their charity. "It is bad enough to find ourselves living with heathen without adopting their outlandish ideas of dress," he said. "These breeches and shirt of mine will serve me well enough."

De Vaca and Castillo eyed him coolly. "Suit yourself," said de Vaca. "For my own part I welcome an opportunity to wear the first strong and comfortable clothes I have known for many weary months."

He changed into Indian costume. Castillo and Esteban did the same. Then a number of pretty young Indian women appeared, dressed in deerskins which reached from shoulder to knee, "garnished very prettily, and ornamented with long fringes of elk's teeth, which are fastened on them in rows." These women brought steaming bowls of dried buffalo meat—probably obtained from the buffalo-hunting Comanche plainsmen to the north—and cooked maize, pumpkins, and beans.

The chieftain of this subtribe was named

Kots-a-to-ah, meaning Smoked Shield. He was nearly seven feet in height and was said to be not only one of the greatest warriors, but the swiftest runner amongst the Comanche people. As a young man he had distinguished himself while staying with his kinsmen on the buffalo-inhabited plains. It was said that he had run down a buffalo on foot and slain it with his lance as he ran by the animal's side.

Kots-a-to-ah made it clear to de Vaca and his companions that he regarded them as honored guests. They were welcome to remain as long as they liked with his people. But his kindly of-fer did not cause the Spaniards any great feeling of pleasure. Although Esteban was soon begin-ning to understand the Indians and join in their hunts for food, his companions were forced to remain in the village. Their European muscles were unfitted for long hours of a chase on foot, and their hands lacked skill with lance and knife. They could not adapt themselves yet to the Indian way of life.

"It causes me to flush with shame," exclaimed Castillo, "when I recall the reputation I once enjoyed as a swordsman, and as a man who could handle prettily both crossbow and arquebus."

"For myself, I am content to learn the simplest native arts first," de Vaca replied. "This morning I helped some women to pound corn— an activity more difficult than it seems, and one which caused me to perspire greatly, besides making the women laugh. Yesterday afternoon I helped an ancient dame to collect and prepare roots and leaves which she declared had magical powers as medicines. Esteban seemed greatly interested in these herbs; possibly he believes in their healing powers."

"Grinding corn and plucking leaves!" Dorantes exclaimed angrily. "Are these proper activities for gentleman soldiers of Spain? Smoke-filled huts, yapping dogs, and fleas! Fine surroundings for men like ourselves! I yearn to quit these natives and their squalid ways."

De Vaca gave Dorantes the blunt answer he

deserved. "We are lucky to be with these people. We must learn what we can from them. We would die if left to our own resources in this wilderness. When we are better equipped with knowledge, we can begin to think of traveling onward to Tampico."

Three weeks later a party of hunters returned to the village, bringing with them eighty stumbling, exhausted, sick, and half-crazy Spaniards. The survivors came from two other barges, which had been hurled onto the coast. For eighteen days they had been living on leaves, birds' eggs, tiny fish caught in pools, and even the grubs they found in rotten timber. Narvaez was not amongst them. Neither he nor the rest of the Spaniards were ever heard of again.

These eighty men threw a heavy strain on the whole village. They took no part in the daily food gathering. The more lowly a Spaniard's origin was, the more loudly he insisted that digging up roots, gathering up roots, gathering maize, and pounding meat was unfitting work for a man. The newcomers could not, or would not, learn to help themselves. They sat in their tents and waited to be fed by the rest of the community. Not even de Vaca, with all his cool commonsense and foresight, could persuade them to lend a hand.

A tremendous storm drenched the island and made it impossible for the Indians to reach the nearby mainland and go hunting. For six days they could neither fish nor dig up the roots on which they relied when other supplies were short. The eighty Spaniards began raiding the Indian tents in search of food, devouring every morsel they could find. This was the only occasion on which de Vaca ever saw Kots-a-to-ah lose his temper. With lance and leveled bow the chieftain's warriors lined up the men who had offended.

"You can leave here if you wish," Kots-a-to-ah said in eloquent sign language, "or you may continue to remain in this village. But if you choose to stay, then you will observe our laws.

The next man who steals from another will be killed."

Disease came to the island during the bitter winter. The Spaniards began sickening and dying. Presently the infectious illness from which they were suffering spread to the Indians. Once again Kots-a-to-ah lined up the Spaniards. This time he included de Vaca and his three companions.

"It seems," began the chieftain, "that this plague came in your bodies to our village. Never before have we suffered from such an illness. We are therefore considering whether we should kill all of you, so that we Indians may become free of the sickness."

De Vaca, ragged and torn, lean and wild-looking in his Indian costume, stood forth to answer for himself and his fellow countrymen.

It was a cause of great wonderment to me that this simple and unlettered Indian should concede us a chance to defend ourselves before ordering that we should be put to death. Had we been in the Indians' place, and they in our own miserable plight, we Spaniards would not have hesitated to destroy them at once. Thus this noble chieftain demonstrated a true lesson in Christianity to ourselves.

De Vaca was a trained and eloquent speaker. He had learned sufficient of the Indian tongue to make himself understood in simple words.

"We were hungry and thirsty when we first came to this village," he said. "But, Chieftain, we were not suffering from any sickness of the kind which now destroys your people and mine. We lived here for three months before the first man died; that is the proof of what I say. Moreover, you have seen me and the tall companion with the black skin plucking roots and herbs daily to prepare medicines by which your people and mine may be cured."

De Vaca's words went straight to the Indian's heart. He was the only Spaniard who could have composed them, for, strange as it may seem, he was the one man amongst them who

[113]

held to his belief that these Indians were human beings like himself. For weeks now he had watched mothers playing with their children, men helping one another in their labors, families sharing their food in friendly manner. These Indians, for all their brown skins and strange beliefs, had much the same nature as the people of Europe. The arguments that would appeal to civilized listeners would surely also appeal to Kots-a-to-ah and his warriors.

De Vaca's belief was justified when the chieftain rose to reply. "You speak the truth," he said. "This plague only came to us after you had dwelt for a long time in our village. It is true that I have seen you and the dark one who sometimes hunts with my own people preparing medicines. Let there be no more talk of killing. I am satisfied."

The cold winds of winter died away. The sea became bright and calm and the sun shone warmly. Spring had returned to Texas and now it was time for the Indians to set out on their annual trip to the mainland. During this expedition they traded with the inland tribes, hunted deer, and procured fresh supplies of dried buffalo meat and pemmican.

Eighteen out of eighty of the second party of Spaniards were still alive in that spring of the year 1530. Most of them were determined to march on toward the west in an effort to reach Tampico. A young Spaniard named Lope de Oviedo, however, a great student of ancient Greek and skilled in the writing of verse, listened to de Vaca's warning.

"The Indians say that dangerous country lies to the west of us. We are not yet sufficiently well-trained in Indian ways, nor are our bodies yet tough enough, to attempt the crossing of that territory. We would be wiser to wait—and to go on waiting."

Alonso del Castillo, Dorantes, and Esteban also agreed with de Vaca's words. Castillo had known the Panama jungles and realized the hardships they would meet on the journey they planned. Dorantes was impatient to move onward, but he had come to respect de Vaca's cool judgment and leadership. Esteban was content to stay. He had become a fair huntsman by this time. Probably he found that his life amongst the Indian warriors compared very favorably with existence amongst his Spanish masters.

The Indians and Spaniards sailed in company to the mainland. There most of the Europeans turned westward and marched across the endless grassy plain until a distant range of low hills hid them from sight. With Kots-a-to-ah and his tribe went de Vaca, Castillo, Dorantes, Esteban, and Oviedo.

The five of them managed to live fairly well throughout the summer. Castillo, who had some skill with a knife, carved little wooden figures and charms from driftwood and exchanged them for food and furs. De Vaca, thanks to his friendship with the old woman witch doctor, was becoming reasonably skilled in the preparation of simple medicines. He began practicing amongst the other tribes with

[116]

whom his party came into contact. Dorantes unwillingly learned to make bone fishhooks, using Castillo's knife for the purpose. He was able to sell his wares without difficulty. Esteban spent most of his time hunting, but also helped de Vaca prepare his herbal remedies. Only Oviedo remained incapable of learning anything. The women treated him with good-natured patience and gave him the simplest tasks to perform.

Back to the island and another cheerless winter went the Indians. De Vaca and the others went with them. There they heard a rumor that the Spaniards who had left had been involved in a fight with another tribe, and that at least some of them had been killed. Certainly none of them was ever heard of again.

"We must wait until the cause of that grievance, whatever it was, has been forgotten," de Vaca told his companions. "Have patience; the day will come when we, too, will march to the west."

They waited for another two years. It was

said that the tribes to the west were at war with one another. Any strangers passing through the country would most likely be killed.

The pipe of peace was smoked in the spring of the year 1532.

"We will start our journey when we reach the mainland," de Vaca said. "Our people will begin their yearly visit within a few weeks."

The day of departure arrived. A fleet of canoes was being filled with all the goods the Indians were taking for barter. Castillo had his usual bundle of cleverly carved wooden figures, Dorantes his stock of fishhooks, Esteban a longbow, and de Vaca his gourds and wooden flasks of medicines.

Oviedo had nothing, not even sufficient courage. The young man burst into sudden tears. "I am afraid to go with you," he confessed. "How can five of us hope to succeed where our other fellow countrymen have failed? These Comanche men and women treat me kindly despite my lack of skills. I have chosen to stay

[118]

with them for the rest of my life rather than risk the journey you have in mind."

They said good-by to him on the beach. No other Spaniards passed that way for a century. Two hundred years later, when the Indians of that region had become ferocious warriors, perhaps some of them had in their veins the proud and cultured blood of poor young Lope de Oviedo of Spain.

## CHAPTER 8

### *Desert Captives*

THAT year the Indians decided to go southward along the coast of Texas. The Spaniards
went with them until they were past the wide
and muddy banks of the Colorado River. There
they said good-by to kindly chief Kots-a-to-ah,
who was now returning northward with his peo-

ple, and continued to go forward by themselves.

For three weeks they plodded and tramped and swam the sandbars and creeks of the muddy coast. The long days of hot sunshine scorched their exposed skins and the sandy ground hardened the soles of their feet. By this time Dorantes had disgustedly thrown away his last remnants of European clothing and thankfully adopted the Indian costume he once despised.

From day to day we have walked under the burning rays of the sun, without more than an occasional small cloud to relieve its intensity, or a bush to shade us, nor did we find anything that even cast a shadow. During this time we discovered many ravines in the beds of which were occasional brackish pools. In these days of cruel marching I had a severe fever which greatly reduced my strength, and the lack of nourishing food weakened me still more.

Somewhere south of the Guadalupe River they came out of the semidesert into picturesque and broken country, with fine springs and

[121]

streams, which afforded them the luxury of cool shade and unlimited water. There they camped for a week.

"I have heard that many parts of Mexico are similar in appearance to this spot," Castillo said hopefully. "Perhaps we are drawing near to Tampico."

"At least we have reached the western coast of the Gulf," de Vaca replied thoughtfully, "for now we are marching south within sight of the sea. A few more days, perhaps, and we will come to some outpost occupied by our fellow countrymen."

They were actually within five hundred miles of Tampico, but the end of their tremendous journey was not yet in sight. Had they known how close they were, they might have hastened onward. Instead they rested beside the shade and the water, catching fish in the streams, eating the flesh of edible lizards which Esteban cooked Indian fashion, and sometimes spearing flounders in the bright sandy-bottomed waters off the nearby coast. They had known so much hunger and met so many hardships during the past five years, that they could enjoy almost anything in the way of food. They roasted fish on stones placed in a fire, pounded pecan nuts in hollow rocks and swallowed them, and regarded a charred mass of eels as an excellent repast. Even Dorantes had come to accept this utterly primitive way of life.

"I recall how in Spain I sometimes found fault with a cook because of some trifling error in the manner in which he had spiced a haunch of venison," he declared. "Yet in this savage country where we wander, I am satisfied to suck the marrow from a burnt bone and eagerly devour a fish's brain and eyes."

"And feel none the worse for it," said del Castillo. "I am forty-seven years of age, and for the past twenty-five of them I have frequently lived for long periods on foods which would cause our fellow countrymen in Spain to shudder in horror and perhaps be sick. Were I to

[123]

feast on the rich dishes of which you speak so wistfully, I warrant an upset stomach would keep me in bed for a month!"

A party of Mariames Indians sighted the smoke of the Spaniards' campfire on the evening of the seventh day. They were dark-skinned and lean-bodied men, with thin, fierce faces and unkindly dispositions. They were

probably a mongrel people containing the blood of many tribes. The Mariames came every year to feast on the ripening nuts which grew on the tall straight pecan trees on the banks of the rivers. Normally they lived far inland in desolate and unpleasant country.

These people took us captive and proceeded to

treat us in a most unkindly manner. We were forced to go with them wheresoever they wandered, and to toil like slaves until we were utterly weary. The Indians gave us heavy burdens to carry and often beat us with rods to hurry our progress.

De Vaca managed somehow to keep his diary in its frayed leather bag—the only item which still served to remind him that once he had been a Spanish gentleman. He studied the Mariames, noting as he wrote that they cast away many of their daughters at birth, and left them to be eaten by dogs.

This period of slavery almost broke the Spaniards' hearts. Month after month went by while they awaited a chance to escape. The summer of 1533 came, and once again the Mariames went to feast in the pecan groves. From there they wandered onward to the southwest, a region where prickly pears could be found. While their captors drank the sweet juice of the prickly pear and squabbled amongst themselves in lazy idleness, the Spaniards still awaited a chance to vanish. None came; at the end of the summer they were forced to return with the Mariames to the dreary interior of Texas.

"Next year we will certainly escape," de Vaca told his despairing companions. "We know now how the Mariames spend their summers, and we are familiar with the country through which we have passed."

Poor Esteban, unable to stand the cruel treatment indefinitely, wrenched a heavy stick from the hand of an Indian who had struck him, and cut the man's head open with a single tremendous blow. For this offense the Mariames thrashed the Negro until he was unconscious, then tied him to a post and left him exposed to the sun from morning to night. The Spaniards nursed Esteban back to health and determined grimly amongst themselves that when the summer of 1534 arrived, nothing would be allowed to prevent their escape.

Their chance came one evening while the moon was rising over the Texan wastes. Some foolish squabble had started amongst the Mari-ames menfolk and the whole tribe was watching and listening to its progress. The three Span-iards and Esteban flitted silently out of the camp. When dawn came, they were twenty miles away and lying hidden amongst the rocks of the coast. There they remained for two days and nights, waiting until they could be reason-ably sure that the detestable Mariames were no longer searching for them. Then, traveling by night for the sake of the coolness, they struck southward again in their never-ending journey toward Tampico.

Somewhere near Corpus Christi Bay they saw another tribe. For a long time the Spaniards lay hidden in a grove of cactus while they gazed at the nearby encampment. Then de Vaca made a risky decision.

"They seem a peaceful people," he said. "The men are sharing the work equally with the women, and there is a lack of weapons amongst them. Let us go forward to meet them."

The Coahuiltecans were a primitive tribe distantly related to the once great Aztec nation. They huddled together to stare at the bearded, long-haired strangers with weather-beaten skins and dressed in frayed Indian costume approaching them. Then realizing that these newcomers meant no harm, they hastened to make friends.

The Coahuiltecans were journeying southward to their own district somewhere in the waste regions between the Nueces River and the Rio Grande. By signs they indicated that there was little water on the way.

"We will go with them," said the fearless de Vaca. "If we must cross a desert to reach Tampico, then let us make the crossing in the company of those who are accustomed to it."

Those glittering wastes of waterless sand formed the most exhausting stage of the Spaniards' whole journey. For five days the plodding tribe with the three gasping, stumbling white men, and the lean, dogged Negro, made their way across that blazing, red-hot country-

[129]

side. Dorantes was the first to become delirious. He began singing loudly and fancied he was at home in his family's mansion in Spain. Then Alonso del Castillo, the brave little soldier, fell down in the sand and cried loudly that he could go no farther because his legs had melted from the heat. De Vaca and Esteban picked him up and consoled him, but that same day the Negro became confused and started babbling in his own African tongue. When evening came, and the tribe halted beside a tiny muddy spring which provided them with scarcely a cup of water each, de Vaca found that he had lost the power of writing. He could remember neither how letters were formed nor how a pen should be held. Yet when a flaming sunrise returned, those three Spaniards and the Negro managed to rise and keep on walking. Theirs was the unbreakable courage and determination that can only be destroyed by death.

They came to water again at the spot where Hebbronville now stands. Late prickly pears were in fruit, and little streams sang and gurgled before losing themselves in the burning sand. Here the Coahuiltecans rested for a while, for they themselves had suffered greatly on the journey across the desert.

De Vaca alone amongst his companions was still fairly clearheaded. Dorantes had not yet fully recovered his senses and often wept hysterically. Castillo had lost his good humor and shouted with nightmares when he slept. Esteban was behaving peculiarly, speaking seldom and often at random, as if his thoughts were utterly scattered.

De Vaca mixed some of the medicines with which he was now familiar and dosed his companions. Perhaps the better food and ample water helped as much as the herbal mixtures to bring the men back to comparative sanity. Overnight de Vaca found that he had acquired amongst the little Mexican Indians a reputation as a great healer. Before long his fame spread in some mysterious way across the desert and

[131]

sick natives were being brought to him daily.

Perhaps de Vaca himself was no longer quite sane. He had a burning faith in himself as a kind of witch doctor and really believed that mysterious powers had been given him by God to cure sick people. The most amazing thing about his work was that he did, incredibly, manage to restore to health a number of Indians who were on the point of death. Seeing these apparent miracles, his three companions were quickly convinced of de Vaca's strange powers. They hastened to learn how to prepare medicines and treat the sick people.

It was indeed fortunate that this gift of healing was bestowed upon us, for otherwise I do not know how we would have lived for so long amongst these poor people. The countryside was destitute of game, and we did not know where to look for food nor by what means it might be obtained. Once when I sought in the desert to find something with which to fill our stomachs, I became utterly lost and remained so for five miserable days. Only by the great goodness of God did I at last find my way back to the place where the Indians were camped. They greeted me in a most joyful manner, saying that they feared I was lost to them for ever.

When the winter season came, the winds blew very coldly. There was now little food to be discovered and famine came to the Indians. Yet they continued to feed us as best they could, in gratitude for the many cures we had effected amongst them. Daily we helped them in searching for wood for the great fire which they kindled every night as comfort against the coldness.

Spring came at last. De Vaca and his three companions were reasonably fit again, but none of them was quite normal in his mind. Esteban had long ago given up showing whatever little interest he may have had in going back to a civilization which meant nothing to him. He was happy to spend his days with a lance and a bow and curl up beside a campfire at night.

Dorantes was silent and inclined to be moody. Sometimes he wept bitterly when he remembered, as in a dream, his idle and aristocratic way of life in Spain. Castillo had been so long in Indian countries that a few extra months, or years, did not worry him greatly. He seemed as interested in helping to cure sick Indians as he was in the prospect of reaching Tampico. De Vaca was still standing up to the trip better than his two Spanish companions, although his earlier life, spent mostly in comfortable and leisurely surroundings, had done little to equip him for the seven years he had spent amongst the tribes of North America. It was only under his continuing leadership that the other men went on traveling toward remote Tampico. De Vaca was also managing to keep a brief record of their wanderings in the last few pages of his crammed and bulky diary.

"It is time for us to start moving again," he said in that spring of the year 1535. "The Coahuiltecans declare that another friendly tribe, not unlike themselves, live to the southwest of this region. It is in the direction in which we wish to go."

[134]

"Then let us start with full bellies," said Dorantes, "for doubtless we shall go hungry again before long. A small dog has been hovering round our hut for the past few nights. It will provide us with a feast."

Esteban caught the dog and killed it. Castillo, who was reckoned the best cook amongst them, grilled the flesh most skillfully on a fire made from dry mesquite wood. Next morning they left the little tribe who for a year had shown them such hospitality. Soon they were trudging across a wide and empty landscape.

"This country has a fairer appearance than the odious deserts we have left behind," del Castillo said. "Last night we found water, bitter but drinkable. This morning Andres had the good fortune to discover a nest of young fledgling birds, which now fill our stomachs adequately. Twenty-four hours and we have gone neither hungry nor thirsty! We even carry an untouched supply of water with us."

"Heavy rain is coming," muttered Esteban,

who had been standing motionless for a moment with his head turned to one side. "I can hear the ground whispering the news, and the air is full of unusual sound."

Wild torrents from a somber sky drenched them that afternoon. The unusual experience was so delightful that they continued to trudge along, singing at the top of their voices. Suddenly they stopped singing to peer into the rain-drenched gloom in front of them. They had come unexpectedly to an Indian village. Dark-faced little people were peering affrightedly from doorways and windows at these shouting apparitions with mud-streaked faces, long hair and beards.

De Vaca's party had reached the Maliacones tribe, whose country extended for a hundred miles to the banks of the Rio Grande. They were now within three hundred and fifty miles of Tampico.

## CHAPTER 9

### *The People of the Pueblos*

"BY the strange manner of your coming," the Indians said to de Vaca, "we know you are great medicine men. It is the custom of this country for all healers to sing strange songs or shake a rattle loudly as they travel."

The Spaniards remained in the village for two

weeks. By day they practiced medicine and apparently again managed to cure a number of the cases brought to them. At night they slept in a small flat-roofed mud hut, "where innumerable lizards and other creatures lived in the shadows of the roof beams and sometimes fell down on us as we slept."

They lived reasonably well during that period. Castillo was right when he said that this country had the appearance of being more fertile. The Maliacones grew scrubby patches of corn and even a few pumpkins. They had large reserves of edible mesquite beans, and ensnared birds provided flesh. It was better fare than the Spaniards had known for months.

The Maliacones had many legends of light-skinned strangers who had come to their land during the past centuries. Children of the Sun they called such visitors, because invariably they came from the west. The Children of the Sun were always honored by the Indians, and such was the case with de Vaca and his companions. When they resumed their march south-ward, guides went with them and messengers traveled ahead to warn other villages that the great white-skinned healers were coming.

At last they came to the Rio Grande and were carried across it in canoes. De Vaca gazed far to the south where, like giant battlements against the clear blue sky, rose the summits of range upon range of mountains. They seemed an utter barrier to further progress. He turned to ask the Maliacones what they knew about these mountains. During the past few months both de Vaca and Esteban had learned to speak the Indian tongue intelligibly.

"We do not know how high the mountains are," the guides replied frankly. "None of our tribe has ever been across them. Perhaps there *is* no way of passing through such great moun-tains."

"At least one would require warmer clothes than we possess for such a journey," said Dor-antes. "These miserable fragments of Indian

[139]

leather we wear would give no protection against the icy mud of high passes."

"And eastward lies the sea," added Castillo. "Last time we went by the coast we fell into the hands of the Mariames. I could not endure such slavery again. Let us turn westward like the Children of the Sun we are supposed to be!"

They did turn toward the sunset, traveling northwest through regions where the Rio Grande tributaries skirted the great desert which was said to lie directly to the south.

Without realizing it, de Vaca had developed into a real explorer. He was no longer a shipwrecked Spanish gentleman seeking civilization. This northwesterly journey through lands where the feet of other white men had never trod became a matter of great interest to him.

De Vaca's little band had been more than seven years in North America. During those seven years they had progressed painfully along the coast of the Mexican Gulf to a point close to the spot where Monterrey now stands. Now, in

1536, the Spaniards began a journey that was to last another two years and covered a distance of two thousand miles. Their route can be followed fairly clearly, but the many tribes they met during that great journey have long since disappeared.

There was no shortage of food in the regions beside the Rio Grande. Flocks of egrets and ibises flew in hundreds over the river. Maize, squash, and pumpkins grew in green, well-watered fields. Villagers were usually able to provide deer meat, or at least rabbit, when they entertained the four Children of the Sun.

Almost worshiped as gods, treated with the greatest awe and respect, wherever they went, it was no wonder that de Vaca and his friends believed more firmly than ever in their divine powers as healers. Esteban procured a copper rattle, the sign of a magician, and wielded it most loudly when approaching a village. De Vaca learned to make new and powerful medicines from deadly herbs, snakes, and the roots

[141]

of poison trees. Castillo had trained himself to become a wonderfully expert carver in wood. Dorantes, whose mind was often filled with queer fancies, fell in love with an attractive Indian girl and informed de Vaca solemnly that he intended to take her to Spain. Esteban was

no longer a frightened African Negro astray in Mexico. He had become a Mexican Indian in thought and ways and speech. Only his hair and features still distinguished him from the local tribesmen.

Seventeen days after setting out on this new

journey, the Spaniards crossed the Rio Grande again near the modern town of El Paso. The count of seventeen days was de Vaca's, but he was probably losing his habit of counting accurately. To have accomplished the journey from Monterrey to El Paso—six hundred miles at least—he and his companions must have covered thirty-five miles a day. But at least they did cross the river again and so came back into Texas. This was the most northerly point they reached during their entire journey.

Now they came to a strange, thirsty, rocky country of great canyons in which stood strange pueblo villages. They were inhabited, so de Vaca declared, by the "most civilized" race they had yet encountered. Ragged, bearded, and burnt black by the sun, the Spaniards held on in a southwesterly direction across this land. Wherever they went, they were treated with the greatest veneration. Perhaps, however, the simple Indians wondered a little why these Children of the Sun should make so many earnest

[144]

enquiries as to where the next water hole lay.

They came at last to the banks of the Yaqui River in Sonora. Gazing down from the barren slopes of the Sierra Madre, where a red-hot wind had emptied their crude water bags and cracked their lips with thirst, they saw sweet green fields and pleasant villages lying below them.

"So must the City of Mexico have appeared to Captain Cortes when he first beheld it," said Dorantes. "A fair and fertile country gleaming in the sunshine, where most succulent crops scented the air with fresh and delicious ripeness."

"Yonder land seems to lack a white-walled splendid city," said Castillo. "No matter. A well-filled plate of savory food will be as welcome to me at this present moment as an empty platter of pure gold. Instead of drinking the Emperor Montezuma's choicest wines, I will be content with an endless draught of cool water."

They stumbled down the slopes of the mountain and came at last to the welcoming plain. It was the nearest de Vaca and his party ever got to finding the legendary country of Cibola, the land of gold, for which, so long ago, the Spaniards had sought.

The large, flat-topped houses of the Indians were cool and dark and gracious. Heavy beams of aromatic timber ran across the ceilings. Strange ornaments hung on the limewashed walls, and on the floors were spread woven mats of the strangest and most intricate design. The Indians dressed in fine cotton garments and the wealthiest amongst them wore ornaments of gold or silver. Sometimes in the evening these kindly people performed strange tribal dances with exquisite rhythm and grace of movement. With a strange lack of interest for any Spaniard to show, de Vaca noted in his diary that the ceremonial arrowheads, which the young people carried as they danced, were inlaid with precious stones. He was much more impressed by the manner in which these Indians received his party.

They gave us very good garments of cotton, so that we were able to cast away the filthy rags we had worn until we came to this land. And when these new clothes became the least soiled, our hosts removed them to be washed and gave us others in their stead. Thus we were no longer nearly naked but able to dress in a much more seemly manner.

During our stay amongst these most friendly people, we were told that sometimes they waged war with their neighbors. When news of our coming reached this country all warfare was abandoned without delay in order that the tribes might have an opportunity to see and welcome the Children of the Sun.

The Spaniards tramped on down the banks of the Sonora River, moving southward from village to village.

"You will come to a great lake whose waters are salt," the Indians told them. "We know nothing of the shores around that lake, for of what use is water that can neither be drunk nor used for the irrigation of crops? The good river which waters our land is of much greater value."

[147]

They came to the sea in the early autumn of the year 1536. From a pleasant, pine-covered hillside they gazed across a sunlit countryside to the bright blue waters of the Gulf of California. De Vaca and his companions had reached the Pacific Ocean from Florida.

"Let us keep away from the coast," said de Vaca. "We know nothing of the tribes who live there, but we do not wish to be taken captive again. Let us merely keep within sight of the coast."

Two hundred miles below the Sonora River, the Spaniards knew at last they were nearing regions inhabited by their fellow countrymen. Villages became fewer and a number were completely deserted. Many of the Indians they saw fled and hid amongst the trees. At the mouth of the flooded Yaqui River, they came across a solitary Indian who saw them too late to run away. Round his neck was a bead necklace from which dangled a Spanish sword-belt buckle.

"Many, many strangers with white skins and

black hair move on the coast far south of here," the Indian told them. "Sometimes they send out great parties of men who kill and burn, torture and destroy. Our people who once lived in this region have fled into other parts to escape from those terrible soldiers. At first I thought you, too, were of the same race as the white-skinned ones. Now I see you are men of some other tribe not unlike my own."

"Where did you find this?" asked de Vaca, touching the sword buckle.

The Indian shrugged. "The White Ones once came north, almost as far as where we now stand. They killed and stole all the time. At last our people gathered together in great numbers amongst yonder hills. Then they came down on the strangers at night and slew them. I was amongst those who fought, and I took this from the dead body of one of those human wolves."

The Indian paused to look at de Vaca and his companions. "I have some dried fish and deer meat in the woods yonder. Tonight I will feed you. Tomorrow you can continue your journey wheresoever you wish."

When we continued our march after hearing this news, we soon perceived for ourselves that the Indian had spoken the truth. Great was our joy to know that we were approaching regions occupied by Spain, yet I must confess to some feeling of shame. We came to many villages which had been destroyed by fire and where we saw many bodies of Indians, women, and children as well as men, who had been killed by our soldiers. My companions and myself grieved to see this destruction wrought by our fellow countrymen.

In March of the year 1537, Cabeza de Vaca, moving slightly ahead of his companions, came out from a grove of trees to gaze across a grassy plain.

A few hundred yards away, he suddenly observed four men sitting motionless on horseback. De Vaca hesitated for a moment, then ran toward them, crying out in Spanish in a trembling voice, and with the tears running down his bearded cheeks. After eight years of wandering, he and his friends had reached the end of their journey across America.

## CHAPTER 10

### *The Royal Court of Spain*

DE VACA's party met their fellow countrymen near the mouth of the River Sinaloa on the
west coast of Mexico. A large band of Spanish
troops was encamped within half a mile of the
meeting place. They were moving under the
command of an unmerciful rogue named Diego
de Alcatraz.

Diego was a slave raider. During his present expedition he had contrived to collect some six hundred Indians up and down the coast. His men were engaged in the usual Spanish occupation of killing, plundering, and burning.

Within a few minutes of the first meeting, Diego realized that this bony, haggard man in tattered cotton clothes and with hair reaching to his shoulders was a person of greatly superior rank to himself. So, for that matter, were Alonso del Castillo and Andres Dorantes. All three bore names that were honored in Spain. Diego de Alcatraz was little more than a very junior officer of obscure family, who had chosen slave raiding as a means to fill his pockets.

"You and your companions are most fortunate, señor," Alcatraz said to de Vaca. "Apart from the seeming miracle which brought you to this area when I happened to be passing through it, I can escort you back to the town of Culiacan almost at once. It is a journey of a mere hundred miles to the south. We have obtained as many slaves as we can comfortably manage."

De Vaca gazed at the poor Indians, men, women, and children, huddled together in scared groups under the guard of armed soldiers. "There is a request I must make of you, Señor Alcatraz," he said slowly. "I ask you to release all those slaves. When we reach Culiacan I can place my hands on sufficient funds to cover the expenses you have been put to in organizing your expedition. I shall compensate you forthwith."

"In Heaven's name, why?" exclaimed Alcatraz. "Should you compensate me merely for my journey, I will lose enormous profit on those human cattle yonder."

"I give you two reasons," de Vaca replied shortly. "Firstly, because it would be an act of thankfulness for a merciful end to our wanderings. Secondly, because for eight years I and my friends have been clothed, housed, and fed by the Indian tribes of America. A few treated us badly, but most treated us well. I do not regard such people as cattle, Señor Alcatraz."

"The same thought was passing through my own head," added Castillo. "It grieves me to see Indians, much the same as those who befriended us, being led away into chained captivity. I, too, can subscribe a fair amount of money to lessen your personal losses, Señor Alcatraz."

"An offer with which I associate myself," said Dorantes. "Though my name is perhaps not well-known in the New World, my family is of some consequence in Spain."

"No," snapped Alcatraz. "I cannot agree with your request. Indians grow more difficult to find with every day that passes. They have fled cunningly into distant parts of the country, where it is almost impossible to find them. These slaves are my property; I fear they must remain so."

"Then," said Cabeza de Vaca briefly, "let us march to Culiacan. I will see the governor of the district."

Governor Melchior Diaz was a cultured and

sensitive gentleman. After greeting de Vaca and his companions in a hospitable manner, Diaz listened to their request.

"I have never believed that the enslavement of others by fear and bloodshed was a practice worthy of our most Christian country," he said. "The slaves brought by Alcatraz shall be released freely and at once. Do not trouble yourselves to reimburse him for his losses. Alcatraz has made a good living out of blood and misery and plunder for the past seven years. He will not dare to complain to higher authority; there are other incidents in his past history which he would not care to have examined too closely."

Six hundred slaves were brought to the gates of the little town and turned loose. Startled and still afraid, they hastened to depart, making for the comparative safety of the distant hills and forests as swiftly as they could.

It is possible that Esteban went with them. There is no record that he went on to Mexico City with his three companions, and it seems likely that he may have chosen to remain with the Indians he liked so well. One rumor has it that Esteban joined later with a Spanish priest in a further hunt for Cibola, but no one knows where or when he died.

In Mexico City, de Vaca, Castillo, and Dorantes were given an enthusiastic welcome by Antonio de Mendoza, the Spanish viceroy. Elegantly dressed and well-fed officials, who had never slept on an uncomfortable bed in their lives, listened in awed silence as the three adventurers told of their incredible experiences. Map makers implored de Vaca to impart what information he could give regarding the coastline and interior districts. Ambitious Spanish officers listened thoughtfully, and undoubtedly with disappointment, as de Vaca declared that nowhere in their tremendous journey had they seen any sign, or even heard a rumor, of the mysterious city of Cibola. His words did more than anything else to discourage Spanish exploration of North America. Of what use was it,

thought the shortsighted Spaniard, to explore and occupy extensive territories if no gold or other precious metals lay in the soil.

De Vaca and Dorantes sailed for Spain in the autumn of 1536. Castillo remained in Mexico. "I have been too long in the New World to

return to the harsh climate of Europe," he declared. "Before long I shall join some other expedition by land or sea. It is in my nature to go on wandering until I grow too old to ride a horse or sleep on a blanket beside a campfire."

De Vaca reached Spain with a great and

brilliant idea in his mind. The king of Spain had granted Panfilo de Narvaez the right to occupy the country of Florida. Narvaez was dead, and Alvar Nuñez de Vera, Cabeza de Vaca, was the only worthy survivor. He was determined to obtain the concession of Florida, and perhaps all the lands of the modern United States for his governorship.

There will be no slavery in those countries, de Vaca thought to himself. The Indians will be taught to trust us, and Spaniards to befriend them. We will preach Christianity kindly to the tribes—not with sword and fire, torture and the whip. I believe that even without gold or silver, that great and splendid land of forest and meadow, desert and river can become a worthy empire of Spain.

De Vaca reached Spain a little too late. Another adventurer had already returned from the New World, lent money to the Spanish king, and obtained from him a grant to occupy and colonize all the lands known as Florida. The adventurer was Hernando de Soto. His body was destined to lie in the depths of the Mississippi River while the battered survivors of his little army roamed hopelessly from Florida to Texas.

"I cannot find other worthy employment for you at present," King Charles said to de Vaca. "You must wait until I have need of you."

There was nothing else for de Vaca to do. He went home to the town of Jerez, to a loyal wife who had never believed her husband was dead, and had looked faithfully after his estate for all those years. There he remained until 1540. In that year he found adventure again.

## CHAPTER 11

### *Jungles of the Gran Chaco*

SPANISH colonists had already settled themselves along the shores at the mouth of the River
Plate, in Argentina. One day their humble
wooden huts and mud-walled forts would give
way to the great city of Buenos Aires. But in
1540 the little colony was struggling to survive.

Few Spanish governors were ever content to
remain at their post and spend their time and

energy building up the economic welfare of a colony. They were always wandering off in search of diamond mines or golden cities, leaving the unfortunate colonists to look after themselves. This was what happened at the Plate River settlement.

Juan de Ayolas was the official governor. First he had led an expedition westward through the terrible swampy jungles of Gran Chaco until they reached the Andes Mountains. There they looted a quantity of silver from a mysterious native tribe and began the homeward march through Paraguay. The Indians caught up with the Spaniards in the jungle and wiped out most of them with poisoned arrows. None of the silver ever reached the settlement on the Plate River.

Ayolas promptly set off on another expedition. The Plate River settlement stood within a few miles of the spot where the giant Parana River flowed into the bay. Ayolas led his men by canoe and barge up this river, between banks covered with tropical forest and inhabited by completely unknown tribes of Indians.

A thousand miles to the north he established a base camp, which he named Asuncion. In command of it he left a tough and unscrupulous officer named Domingo de Irala. Ayolas himself, accompanied by a strong party of troops, carried on up the river in his crazy but fearless search for a silver city.

Cabeza de Vaca was summoned to appear at the royal palace at Seville. A high council of statesmen placed before him all these facts concerning the Plate River settlement.

"The colonists have petitioned our most gracious Majesty," they said. "Perhaps with some truth they declare that they are being neglected by their governor. Indeed, they seem to think Señor Ayolas will never return from his attempt to pass through the Gran Chaco—which is seemingly a great jungle—by river. They appear equally convinced that should Señor Domingo de Irala become governor instead, many of them will be hanged. The colonists request that a new governor be appointed forthwith, one who will devote his attention to restoring the settlement to good order. His Majesty has directed us to inform you that you are to be the new governor of the Plate River settlement. But should Governor Ayolas ever return from his jungle in sane and healthy condition, then you will continue to serve under him as Lieutenant-Governor."

Cabeza de Vaca sailed for South America in the summer of 1541. He was now forty-eight years old, an age at which most men in those days were beginning to think of spending their last few years of life in comfort. But de Vaca was no soft-living courtier existing on rich food and heavy wines.

Those years in North America had given his spare frame a wiry and tireless strength. His body was so deeply tanned that even after three years in Europe he remained almost as dark-skinned as an Indian. Even his somewhat gaunt features had developed a curiously Indian appearance. His eyes had become slightly oblique —perhaps from constant exposure to a blinding sun—and he had the typical, high-bridged nose of the North American tribesmen. Moreover, he had developed a habit of silence and impassive thought, which upset his naturally gay and talkative fellow countrymen.

"He is an uneasy fellow to have in one's company," they declared. "Is it possible that when he lived amongst the Indians, his nature changed until it became like theirs."

One habit of de Vaca's had not changed with the passing of years. He still kept a diary. As his liking for little-known places continued to grow, so did the length and interest of his entries increase.

The squadron in which de Vaca sailed meandered across the Atlantic Ocean in the erratic fashion of those days. Off the coast of Brazil they almost ran ashore in the darkness.

We were only saved from destruction on the

rocks by the presence of a cricket aboard our lead-ing vessel. This little insect chirped most loudly, knowing that land was near. On hearing its loud note, we put about forthwith and, having lowered our sails, remained far out to sea until daylight re-turned.

Dawn brought something else besides a view of the nearby coast. Across the ocean came a lit-tle bark filled with twenty desperate men.

"We are from the Plate River settlement," they told de Vaca, when he ordered them to be brought aboard his vessel. "Already we have sailed a thousand miles north to escape from it. Our governor, Juan de Ayolas, is reported by the natives to have been murdered far up the Parana River. Señor Irala still remains at Asun-cion. It is said that he is surrounded by native tribes in the jungle, who every day grow more hostile toward him. We sailed in the bark be-cause we prefer to risk our lives in an attempt to reach Spain rather than remain any longer in a sick and poverty-ridden colony."

[167]

That evening de Vaca called a meeting of the officers under his command. He had come to a decision that was to send him on the second great exploring expedition of his life.

"If we continue to sail south to the Plate River," he said, "a year—perhaps longer—must pass before we can rescue Irala by moving up the Parana River. It seems that at present we are almost in the same latitude as his camp at the place called Asuncion. We will land an expedition, and march across country to reach him."

The officers were almost too shocked to reply. Those who had not been in South America were horrified at the thought of tramping countless miles through tropical forests, where they would be exposed to many unknown perils. The men who had been in Brazil previously were equally scared. They knew something of the tribes who lived in that steaming, rain-soaked forest and fought with poisoned arrows. They remembered the fevers, the clinging, blood-

BRAZIL

MATO GROSSO

March 1543 de Vaca turns back

R. Taquari

SWAMP

BOLIVIA

Paraguay River

R. Pilcomayo

Asuncion

March 1542

Pacific Ocean

CHILE

GRAN CHACO

PARAGUAY

Territory of the Chaco

Parana River

Uruguay River

Nov 1541

Santa Catarina

URUGUAY

ARGENTINA

Buenos Aires

R. Plate

de Vaca sails to Spain March 1545

South Atlantic Ocean

0   100   200   300   400 Miles

thirsty leeches, the damp that rotted the stout-
est clothing, and the ever-present danger of
being utterly lost in poisonous swamps.

De Vaca listened thoughtfully to the agitated
protests of his officers. He was not impressed.
All those dangers his companions spoke about
were dangers he had met before. "We will begin our march as soon as an expedition can be
put ashore and native guides employed," he
declared.

The Spaniards stared in astonishment at de
Vaca as soon as they reached the land. Alone
and unarmed he wandered off into the forest,
moving lightly and carelessly as if he were fully
accustomed to the South American jungle. Anxious followers discovered him an hour later. He
was seated in a primitive Indian village, making
friends in sign language with a crowd of fearsome bush warriors.

A week later de Vaca was friendly with the
whole tribe. By time he had even acquired
some knowledge of their clicking and swift-

running language. "These men will be our guides," he said. "Now we are ready to march."

On November 22, 1541, the unhappy expedition entered the jungle. Two hundred and fifty officers and soldiers marched behind de Vaca and his little band of Indians. The Spaniards were more scared than ever. They were beginning to believe that de Vaca was completely mad. Never before had they heard such strange orders as those he issued before the journey began.

"No man shall loot or take anything belonging to an Indian. No native house or other building shall be damaged in any way, nor shall it be occupied except with the owner's permission. All foodstuffs shall be honestly bought by those officers whom I have appointed for the purpose. No other Spaniard shall barter or otherwise traffic with any Indian. Any soldier who strikes or injures any native, except in self-defense, shall be hanged if found guilty."

In those orders, de Vaca set a new code of be-

havior for the men of Spain. Had other Spanish explorers and adventurers laid down similar
rules, the entire history of their country's
achievements in the New World would have
made a glittering and wonderful record. Instead, Spain always tried to conquer by sword
and fire and bloodshed. It was a process that
eventually cost her every foot of the New World
she had once occupied, and left her in the end
with nothing. But civilized de Vaca was too
many centuries ahead of his countrymen for
them to consider him anything but crazy.

Over the coastal mountains and into the forests of the interior went the Spaniards. Nine-
teen days after leaving the coast they came to a
stretch of open country. Guarani tribesmen
brought great baskets of maize, live chickens,
and coconuts. In some mysterious way the
natives knew already that they would be fairly
treated.

The troops ate as much as they wanted. Even
the veterans declared wonderingly that never

before had they fared so well in this country. Perhaps one or two intelligent fellows amongst them began to wonder if perhaps de Vaca was right. But the great majority of Spaniards merely laughed at his unceasing efforts to establish friendship with these naked savages.

"He takes himself for an Indian," they whispered. "Perhaps his brain was touched by the hardships of Florida. Instead of taking freely what food we require from the fields, he barters for it with mirrors and cloth, iron nails and needles."

The open country was left behind. The Spaniards entered the forest again, tramping along trails cut by obliging Indians. Maize, honey, deer, and birds were brought to the camp daily, and the Spaniards feasted where under any other leader they would have starved and died —or been murdered.

Five hundred miles from the coast the forest again thinned out. Ahead lay a range of barren mountains, never thoroughly explored to this day. The Spaniards shivered as they climbed through the passes; the thin air seemed bitingly cold after the steamy heat of the jungle they had just passed through.

De Vaca still held his place at the head of the marching column. The everlasting dampness had reduced the men's shoes to sodden and pulpy masses of leather. Their feet were becoming sore and lacerated by the thongs with which they were compelled to secure the remnants of leather to their soles. De Vaca merely threw his shoes away. He walked barefoot, with the Indian guides trotting alongside him. The mounted cavaliers may have smiled a little contemptuously at him, but the stumbling soldiers were highly envious. They would not have believed that any Christian gentleman could go barefoot across such terrible ground.

Over the mountains and down into fresh jungle walked de Vaca. They came to a great Indian village, where the cooking pots were already filled with the savory flesh of armadillos and wild boars. The natives were the most primitive and fearsome the Spaniards had ever seen. They crossed themselves and shuddered when warriors whose necks were decorated with necklaces of human finger bones clustered round de Vaca and showed him every sign of friendship. Later those same Spaniards discovered that the meat tasted as good as it smelled. Famished after their chilly crossing of the mountains, they gorged themselves that night.

The next stretch of jungle was denser, darker, and more dangerous than anything the Spaniards had yet encountered. In the uncertain green twilight of its depths they saw animals stranger than anything they had ever imagined. Huddled round campfires at night they heard the eerie cries of unknown wild beasts, and stared uncomfortably into the darkness at slinking tawny forms whose eyes glowed yellow in the firelight.

"Our leader has indeed gone mad," exclaimed

the frightened men. "He takes himself for a god in this land and strides through these awesome forests in search of Indian tribes to worship him."

With those unfaltering, faithful guides, de Vaca found his way through the wilderness of Paraguay. At last his haggard and ragged followers saw the forest thinning out ahead of them. Beyond it they perceived the bright glow of a great river. Out from the forest they came to find open plains basking in the clear sunshine. They had reached the banks of the Parana River.

"We will halt here for ten days," de Vaca ordered. "There will be food enough for all of us in this grassy country. Let every man take part in the finding of it."

The Spaniards hunted deer and peccary and wild boar, using crossbow and arquebus and lance to bring down their game. They washed their filthy garments in the river, basked in the sunshine, built comfortable reed huts for themselves, and glanced with perplexed eyes at their silent, brooding leader.

De Vaca now led his men northward, moving parallel to the great river. A hundred miles from where they had made camp, they came face to face with a wild horde of forest tribesmen, drawn up across the path they must follow. The Spaniards hesitated uneasily while they fidgeted with their weapons. They feared no foe who fought cleanly, but they were mortally scared of those wicked little arrows whose sharp barbs were tinged brown with poison. Once that venom entered a man's flesh, his blood turned black and his whole body grew rigid. Nothing could save him from death within a few hours.

De Vaca walked forward to meet the warriors. The dark-faced, scowling Indians stared curiously at the lonely figure approaching them. His sharp-featured face was not unlike their own, his hair was of equal length, and his skin was scarcely lighter than theirs. Moreover, this

[177]

strange man bore splendid gifts in his hands and called out to them loudly in their own tongue.

Grumbling and somewhat shamefaced, the Indians laid aside their wicked little bows and venom-tipped lances. They surrounded de Vaca, uttering strange exclamations of delight as they took the gifts from his outstretched hands. Instead of murdering the Spaniards, they befriended them. After pausing to prepare a feast, a number took their place at the head of the column and continued to guide de Vaca northward. Soon they came to the *llanos,* the vast level plains of South America, which were rich and fragrant with flowers at that season. The Spaniards gazed astonished at such loveliness in the heart of this dark continent they feared so greatly.

At nine o'clock in the morning of March 11, 1542, Cabeza de Vaca walked into Asuncion. In less than five months he had led his expedition across a thousand miles of country, where

[178]

no other white man's foot had ever trod. During the entire journey not a single Spaniard had lost his life as the result of hostile action by any Indian.

## CHAPTER 12

### *End of the Road*

DOMINGO DE IRALA, the commander at Asuncion, was still alive. He was a typical Spanish officer, cruel, courteous, courageous, and a bully. Although delighted to be rescued from the dangerous position in which his garrison had placed themselves by their bad treatment of the surrounding tribes, he disliked having to hand over his authority to de Vaca.

"Even with the men you have brought, these accursed Indians are too strong for us to go up-river in search of Governor Ayolas," he declared. "They will waylay our soldiers and kill them."

"Then let us try to make peace with the Indians," suggested de Vaca, and proceeded to do so.

Prisoners held in the camp and used unmercifully as slaves were freed. The Spanish troops were ordered to make no more raids on villages deep in the forests. Under de Vaca's supervision, those Indians who appeared were kindly treated and encouraged to bring supplies of food. Three months later, warfare between the Spaniards and the natives had utterly ceased. Word had spread through the jungle that a new and kindly leader was in charge of the fort.

"Now we can try sending an expedition up-river," said de Vaca. "I will sail with it myself."

Ten heavy boats containing four hundred men began the ascent of the Parana. Sometimes

they had to land and make portages; sometimes they rowed and floundered through long
stretches of swamp. The men grumbled, but
they were held together by de Vaca's firm discipline, in which, despite themselves, they were
coming to believe.

"No robbing of native crops," he ordered.
"No entering of native houses or mistreatment
of the natives."

Unknown tribes appeared from the forest to
stare at the white-skinned strangers. They
brought a medicinal tree bark to cure the fever-
stricken men, turkeys and wild boar to feed
them. They put aside their bows and lances to
seat themselves beside de Vaca and gaze at the
little presents he handed them. The day came
when these silent, usually hostile Indians gave
the information that put an end to the search.

"The white man you seek is dead," they told
him. "He died of fever in the forest not far from
here."

There was no point in de Vaca continuing his

voyage. Perhaps he should have hastened to return to Asuncion and the waiting Captain Domingo de Irala. Instead, he gazed northward across the never-ending land of forest and river, where no white man had ever gone. His curiosity as an explorer was aroused; perhaps he felt more at home in the jungle with the Indians than he did in the more civilized company of Spaniards. Somewhere in that green fever-laden jungle a great lost city or, as Indian rumor stated, a strange white-skinned tribe might be awaiting discovery. The temptation was too great for de Vaca to resist.

"We will go on northward," he said. "Our boats will carry us up this nearby tributary of the Parana which is called the Paraguay River."

He led his clumsy little fleet through six hundred miles of the most difficult and dangerous country in the world. North they went through the swamplands of Brazil until they gazed upon the slime-green waters of the Taquary River. The jungle lay all around them. Huge crocodiles sprawled on the sunny mudbanks in the river, hunting jaguars howled throughout the night, and lumbering, foolish sloths blundered in amongst the sleeping men.

De Vaca was still not satisfied. Urged on by the restless curiosity of the born explorer, he continued through vast mosquito-haunted swamps and past stretches of firm ground where great anthills towered offshore. The startled Spaniards met devil-worshiping Indians, shuddered as they gazed at shrunken human heads, and cursed the great vampire bats which sucked their blood while they slept.

Perhaps, as his companions suggested, de Vaca really was a little mad. More likely his years of wandering in North America had left him completely unafraid of hardship and danger. No sooner had his laboring boats reached Lake Gaiba on the frontier between Bolivia and Brazil, than he suggested leaving them behind and traveling westward overland.

How far he might have gone in that direction

remains a matter of doubt. He might have become the first European to cross South America from coast to coast. It would have been a terrible and almost impossible journey, yet such was de Vaca's extraordinary power over the Indians that perhaps he could have accomplished it. But the Spaniards with him were ordinary professional soldiers and adventurers, devoid of any great interest in exploration, except in search of gold. They stared at the dripping green forest, the giant canebrakes, and the sodden ground beneath their feet. The month of March in 1543 had arrived, bringing with it the season of roaring, tropical rains. Seven months had passed since they left Asuncion. Their armor was rusty, their clothes in rags, and their bodies were shivering with fever. Brave men though they were, they refused to travel onward.

"Nearly a thousand miles of nightmare swamp and river and forest lie between us and our isolated companions at Asuncion," they said.

"From Asuncion to the mouth of the Plate River is perhaps another thousand miles. We have done enough! We will not go forward another mile!"

By the time they reached Asuncion again, in July 1543, the Spaniards were indignant with de

Vaca for the iron restraint he had kept on them. They deeply resented being ordered to treat primitive Indians in a fair and courteous manner. They would have preferred to torture those same natives to wrest information from them regarding nearby countries wherein might lie great treasures of gold and silver. Seldom could any Spaniards bring themselves to realize that not all regions of the New World were filled with wealth. Once they were safely back behind the wooden stockades of Asuncion, the Spaniards who had gone with de Vaca ungratefully forgot that he alone had preserved their lives from the Indians.

Domingo de Irala, a conceited officer, was incapable of showing any more gratitude. De Vaca had succeeded where he himself had failed. Indians turned their backs and slipped away when they saw Irala approaching. They came forward with smiling faces and outstretched hands to meet de Vaca. But Irala was a cunning individual. He allowed de Vaca to guide the whole expedition safely down the remaining reaches of the Parana River to the Plate River settlement on the coast, before making an attempt to ruin him.

The accusations which Irala framed against de Vaca were handsomely set out on parchment and signed by colonists who were afraid to do otherwise. No modern court of law would have regarded the charges as anything except malicious nonsense.

De Vaca had insisted on buying all food supplies from the Indians and had, therefore, made a large and illegal profit for himself. So said Irala. De Vaca had encouraged the devil-worshiping tribe and even taken part in their sacrilegious ceremonies. He had used his men with great hardship. He had concealed information from them regarding a wealthy Indian city in which lay much gold. He had encouraged slaves to revolt against their masters.

High Spanish officials read these extraordinary statements with confused thoughts. They were slowly beginning to realize that Spanish colonists were an ungovernable lot. Sooner or later they were always bound to start plotting against even the best governor that Spain could provide. Yet something had to be done about this petition from the River Plate settlement.

To ignore it would start fresh troubles amongst the colonists.

De Vaca was ordered to return to Spain in order that his actions might be examined fully. He sailed from the River Plate in March, 1545, when he was fifty-two years old.

What happened after de Vaca reached Spain was much the same as what happened to Balboa, Cortes, Pizarro, and other great Spanish explorers. They were all publicly disgraced and deprived of office, or simply murdered. But at least de Vaca was more fortunate than most of his contemporaries. He was merely imprisoned for three years, forbidden to visit the Americas again after his release, and promptly forgotten by a country which seldom showed anything but jealousy, ingratitude, and hatred toward its greatest men.

In 1557, Alvar Nuñez de Vera, Cabeza de Vaca, died peacefully in the little Spanish cathedral town of Valladolid.

**THE END**

RONALD SYME spent his boyhood in New Zealand, sailing and hunting wild boar much of the time. At sixteen, he left school and went to sea in a Pacific cargo steamer, and for four years he traded between Australia, New Zealand, San Francisco, and the South Sea Islands. At eighteen, he began writing short stories, and in 1934 he left the sea to become a professional writer.

During World War II Mr. Syme served in the British Merchant Service as a gunner until he was transferred to the British Army Intelligence Corps because he spoke four foreign languages. He also fought with the Eighth Army in Africa and became a paratrooper during the Italian campaign.

Today Mr. Syme is a well-known author in both England and the United States. An insatiable voyager, he still continues to visit various portions of the globe, for research or pleasure. He recently sailed 1660 miles in a twenty-ton schooner from New Zealand to Rarotonga in the Cook Islands.